notes from a small room

Ruskin Bond
25/8/09

BOOKS BY THE AUTHOR

Fiction
The Room on the Roof & Vagrants in the Valley
The Night Train at Deoli and Other Stories
Time Stops at Shamli and Other Stories
Our Trees Still Grow in Dehra
A Season of Ghosts
When Darkness Falls and Other Stories
A Flight of Pigeons
Delhi Is Not Far
A Face in the Dark and Other Hauntings
The Sensualist
A Handful of Nuts

Non-fiction
Rain in the Mountains
Scenes from a Writer's Life
The Lamp Is Lit
The Little Book of Comfort
Landour Days

Anthologies
Dust on the Mountain: Collected Stories
The Best of Ruskin Bond
Friends in Small Places
Indian Ghost Stories (ed.)
Indian Railway Stories (ed.)
Classical Indian Love Stories and Lyrics (ed.)
Tales of the Open Road
Ruskin Bond's Book of Nature
Ruskin Bond's Book of Humour
A Town Called Dehra

Poetry
Ruskin Bond's Book of Verse

notes from a small room

Ruskin Bond

PENGUIN BOOKS

PENGUIN BOOKS

Published by the Penguin Group

Penguin Books India Pvt. Ltd, 11 Community Centre, Panchsheel Park,
New Delhi 110 017, India

Penguin Group (USA) Inc., 375 Hudson Street, New York, New York 10014, USA

Penguin Group (Canada), 90 Eglinton Avenue East, Suite 700, Toronto,
Ontario, M4P 2Y3, Canada (a division of Pearson Penguin Canada Inc.)

Penguin Books Ltd, 80 Strand, London WC2R 0RL, England

Penguin Ireland, 25 St Stephen's Green, Dublin 2, Ireland
(a division of Penguin Books Ltd)

Penguin Group (Australia), 250 Camberwell Road, Camberwell,
Victoria 3124, Australia (a division of Pearson Australia Group Pty Ltd)

Penguin Group (NZ), 67 Apollo Drive, Rosedale, North Shore 0632,
New Zealand (a division of Pearson New Zealand Ltd)

Penguin Group (South Africa) (Pty) Ltd, 24 Sturdee Avenue, Rosebank,
Johannesburg 2196, South Africa

Penguin Books Ltd, Registered Offices: 80 Strand, London WC2R 0RL, England

First published by Penguin Books India 2009

Copyright © Ruskin Bond 2009

Cover photograph by Ruskin Bond

10 9 8 7 6 5 4 3 2 1

ISBN 9780143067450

Typeset in Footlight MT Light by SÜRYA, New Delhi
Printed at Chaman Offset Printer, Delhi

contents

contents

acknowledgements

Over the years, many of these pieces were published in *The Lady* (London), *The Christian Science Monitor* (Boston), *Deccan Herald* (Bangalore), *The Tribune* (Chandigarh), *Assam Tribune* (Guwahati), *The Telegraph* (Calcutta), *Sun* (New Delhi), *Swagat* (New Delhi) and *Lokmat Times* (Nagpur). A few have lain dormant in my notebooks and have not been published before. Others are more recent. With the exception of nine or ten personal favourites, this is the first time the magazine articles are appearing between book covers.

introduction

Shortly after I had finished writing 'Thoughts on Reaching 75', which rounds off this collection of essays, I remembered that forty-five years ago I had written a piece called 'Thoughts on Reaching Thirty', which had appeared in a couple of papers. I decided I would try to find a clipping of that old article, just to see if my thoughts at that time were radically different from what they are today. So I rummaged in my drawers and cupboards, looking for old scrapbooks and files, but I couldn't find the article. Lost, like so many others. Not that it mattered. My thoughts at the time could not have been very brilliant or original. If they had been worth preserving, I would have saved the article!

What I did find during my hunt was a bunch of old magazines, back numbers of *The Lady*, a British weekly to which I had contributed articles and essays of a personal and anecdotal nature over a period of several years, when I was in my thirties and forties. And flipping through them, I came across several 'lost' pieces—articles which had not appeared again, either in magazines or between book covers, and which I was now happy to see after so many years— 'A Year with Suzie', 'To See a Tiger', 'When Time Stands Still', and others—pieces which would be unfamiliar to my readers.

I have added them to this collection of new essays and a few old favourites of mine. The shorter pieces, such as 'Geraniums', 'Solitude', 'Catch a Moonbeam', etc., are taken from my diary and notebooks up till last year, and have not been published before. Others, such as 'Remember This Day', 'Something to Celebrate' and 'Those Simple Things', have appeared recently in the magazine supplements of some of our newspapers.

Whether written yesterday or long ago, they have a few things in common—a love of books, of kindly people, of the endless fascination of nature, of the wide-eyed wonder of children, of the sights, sounds and scents of a country that never runs out of surprises.

I have made no attempt at chronology. My writing hasn't changed much over the years. That's because I haven't changed. I am still the impractical dreamer that I was sixty years ago, when I decided that writing would be my vocation and my profession.

I do not suffer from writer's block. I have only to sit down at my desk for the words to come tumbling on to my writing pad. And if an ant moves across my desk, I shall record its transit. The world may be in a state of financial and political turmoil, but that doesn't mean ants should stop going about their business. Ants are determined creatures, who will be in the sugar-bowl no matter how high on the shelf you place it.

I keep my old typewriter for sentimental reasons, but now I do all my writing by hand. I have nothing against computers, but I like the feel of paper and I like watching the ink flow from my pen. As long as my fingers are still firm, why not use them?

There is something sensual, physical, intimate about writing by hand. It takes me back to my childhood, when I was first learning to write letters and join them together. When I had any difficulty, my father would put his hand on mine and guide it along the page.

His hand is still there. I feel it now, even as I write.

And may loving, long-gone hands touch yours, dear reader.

We are not alone.

24 April 2009   RUSKIN BOND

those simple things

It's the simple things in life that keep us from going crazy.

Like that pigeon in the skylight in the New Delhi Nursing Home where I was incarcerated for two or three days. Even worse than the illness that had brought me there were the series of tests that the doctors insisted I had to go through—gastroscopies, endoscopies, X-rays, blood tests, urine tests, probes into any orifice they could find, and at the end of it all a nice fat bill designed to give me a heart attack.

The only thing that prevented me from running

into the street, shouting for help, was that pigeon in the skylight. It sheltered there at various times during the day, and its gentle cooing soothed my nerves and kept me in touch with the normal world outside. I owe my sanity to that pigeon.

Which reminds me of the mouse who shared my little bed-sitting room in London, when I was just seventeen and all on my own. Those early months in London were lonely times for a shy young man going to work during the day and coming back to a cold, damp, empty room late in the evening. In the morning I would make myself a hurried breakfast, and at night I'd make myself a cheese or ham sandwich. This was when I noticed the little mouse peeping out at me from behind the books I had piled up on the floor, there being no bookshelf. I threw some crumbs in his direction, and he was soon making a meal of them and a piece of cheese. After that, he would present himself before me every evening, and the room was no longer as empty and lonely as when I had first moved in. He was a smart little mouse and sometimes he would speak to me—sharp little squeaks to remind me it was dinner time.

Months later, when I moved to another part of London, I had to leave him behind—I did not want to deprive him of friends and family—but it was a fat little mouse I left behind.

During my three years in London I must have lived in at least half-a-dozen different lodging houses, and the rooms were usually dull and depressing. One had a window looking out on a railway track; another provided me with a great view of a cemetery. To spend my day off looking down upon hundreds of graves was hardly uplifting, even if some of the tombstones were beautifully sculpted. No wonder I spent my evenings watching old Marx Brothers films at the Everyman Cinema nearby.

Living in small rooms for the greater part of my life, I have always felt the need for small, familiar objects that become a part of me, even if sometimes I forget to say hello to them. A glass paperweight, a laughing Buddha, an old horseshoe, a print of Hokusai's *Great Wave*, a suitcase that has seen better days, an old school tie (never worn, but there all the same), a gramophone record (can't play it now, but when I look at it, the song comes back to me), a potted fern, an old address-book ... Where have they gone, those old familiar faces? Not one address is relevant today (after some forty years), but I keep it all the same.

I turn to a page at the end, and discover why I have kept it all these years. It holds a secret, scribbled note to an early love:

'I did not sleep last night, for you had kissed me. You held my hand and put it to your cheek and to your breasts. And I had closed your eyes and kissed them, and taken your face in my hands and touched your lips with mine. And then, my darling, I stumbled into the light like a man intoxicated, and did not say or know what people were saying or doing . . .'

Gosh! How romantic I was at thirty! And reading that little entry, I feel like going out and falling in love again. But will anyone fall in love with an old man of seventy-five?

Yes! There's a little mouse in my room.

a good philosophy

The other day, when I was with a group of students, a bright young thing asked me, 'Sir, what is your philosophy of life?'

She had me stumped.

There I was, a seventy-five-year-old, still writing, and still functioning physically and mentally (or so I believed), but quite helpless when it came to formulating 'a philosophy of life'.

How dare I reach the venerable age of seventy-five without a philosophy; without anything resembling a religious outlook; without arming myself with a battery of great thoughts with which to impress my young interlocutor, who is obviously in need of a little practical if not spiritual guidance to help her navigate the shoals of life.

This morning I was pondering on this absence of a philosophy or religious outlook in my make-up, and feeling a little low because it was cloudy and dark outside, and gloomy weather always seems to dampen my spirits. Then the clouds broke up and the sun came out, large, yellow splashes of sunshine in my room and upon my desk, and almost immediately I felt an uplift of spirit. And at the same time I realized that no philosophy would be of any use to a person so susceptible to changes in light and shade, sunshine and shadow. I was a pagan, pure and simple; a sensualist; sensitive to touch and colour and fragrance and odour and sounds of every description; a creature of instinct, of spontaneous attractions, given to illogical fancies and attachments. As a guide, philosopher and friend I am of no use to anyone, least of all to myself.

I think the best advice I ever had was contained in these lines from Shakespeare which my father had copied into one of my notebooks when I was nine years old:

'This above all, to thine own self be true,
And it must follow as the night of the day,
Thou can'st not then be false to any man.'

a good philosophy

Each one of us is a mass of imperfections, and to be able to recognize and live with our imperfections, our basic natures, defects of genes and birth—hereditary flaws—makes for an easier transit on life's journey.

I am always a little wary of saints and godmen, preachers and teachers, who are ready with solutions for all our problems. For one thing, they talk too much. When I was at school, I mastered the art of sleeping (without appearing to sleep) through a long speech or lecture by the principal or visiting dignitary, and I must confess to doing the same thing today. The trick is to sleep with your eyes half closed; this gives the impression of concentrating very hard on what is being said, even though you might well be roaming happily in dreamland.

In our imperfect world there is far too much talk and not enough thought.

The TV channels are awash with TV gurus telling us how to live, and they do so at great length. This verbal diarrhoea is infectious and appears to affect newspersons and TV anchors who are prone to lecturing and bullying the guests on their shows. Too many know-alls. A philosophy for living? You won't find it on your TV sets. You will learn more from a cab driver or street vendor.

'And what's *your* philosophy?' I asked my *sabziwalla*, as he weighed out a kilo of onions.

'Philosophy? What's that?' He turned to his assistant. 'Is this gentleman trying to abuse me?'

'No, sir,' I said. 'It's not a term of abuse. I was just asking—are you a happy man?'

'Why do you want to know? Are you from the income-tax department?'

'No, I'm just a storyteller. So tell me—what makes you happy?'

'A good customer,' he said. 'So tell me—what makes *you* happy?'

'The same thing, I suppose,' I had to confess. 'A good publisher!'

I did not tell him about the sunshine, the bird-song, the bedside book, the potted geranium, and all the other little things that make life worth living. It's better that he finds out for himself.

remember this day

If you can get an entire year off from school when you are nine years old, and can have a memorable time with a great father, then that year has to be the best time of your life even if it is followed by sorrow and insecurity.

It was the result of my parents' separation at a time when my father was on active service in the R.A.F. during World War II. He managed to keep me with him for a summer and winter, at various locations in New Delhi—Hailey Road, Atul Grove Lane, Scindia House—in apartments he had rented, as he was not permitted to keep a child in the quarters assigned to service personnel. This arrangement suited me perfectly, and I had a wonderful year in Delhi, going to the cinema, quaffing milkshakes, helping my father with his stamp collection; but this idyllic situation could not continue for ever, and when my father was transferred to Karachi he had no option but to put me in a boarding school.

This was the Bishop Cotton Preparatory School in Simla—or rather, Chhota Simla—where boys studied up to Class 4, after which they moved on to the senior school.

Although I was a shy boy, I had settled down quite well in the friendly atmosphere of this little school, but I did miss my fathers' companionship, and I was overjoyed when he came up to see me during the midsummer break. He had a couple of days' leave, and he could only take me out for a day, bringing me back to school in the evening.

I was so proud of him when he turned up in his dark blue R.A.F. uniform, a Flight Lieutenant's stripes very much in evidence as he had just been promoted. He was already forty, engaged in Codes and Ciphers and not flying much. He was short and stocky, getting bald, but smart in his uniform. I gave him a salute—I loved giving salutes—and he returned the salutation and followed it up with a hug and a kiss on my forehead.

'And what would you like to do today, son?'

'Let's go to Davico's,' I said.

Davico's was the best restaurant in town, famous for its meringues, marzipans, curry-puffs and pastries.

So to Davico's we went, where of course I gorged myself on confectionery as only a small schoolboy can do.

'Lunch is still a long way off, so let's take a walk,' suggested my father. And provisioning ourselves with more pastries, we left the Mall and trudged up to the Monkey Temple at the top of Jakko Hill. Here we were relieved of the pastries by the monkeys, who simply snatched them away from my unwilling hands, and we came downhill in a hurry before I could get hungry again. Small boys and monkeys have much in common.

My father suggested a rickshaw ride around Elysium Hill, and this we did in style, swept along by four sturdy young rickshaw-pullers. My father took the opportunity of relating the story of Kipling's *Phantom Rickshaw* (this was before I discovered it in print), and a couple of other ghost stories designed to build up my appetite for lunch.

We ate at Wenger's (or was it Clark's?) and then—

11

'Enough of ghosts, Ruskin. Let's go to the pictures.'

I loved going to the pictures. I know the Delhi cinemas intimately, and it hadn't taken me long to discover the Simla cinemas. There were three of them—the Regal, the Ritz, and the Rivoli.

We went to the Rivoli. It was down near the ice-skating ring and the old Blessington Hotel. The film was about an ice-skater and starred Sonja Henie, a pretty young Norwegian Olympic champion who appeared in a number of Hollywood musicals. All she had to do was skate and look pretty, and this she did to perfection. I decided to fall in love with her. But by the time I'd grow up and finished school she'd stopped skating and making films! Whatever happened to Sonja Henie?

After the picture it was time to return to school. We walked all the way to Chhota Simla, talking about what we'd do during the winter holidays, and where we would go when the War was over.

'I'll be in Calcutta now,' said my father. 'There are good bookshops there. And cinemas. And Chinese restaurants. And we'll buy more gramophone records, and add to the stamp collection.'

It was dusk when we walked slowly down the path to the school gate and playing-field. Two of my friends were waiting for me—Bimal and Riaz. My father spoke to them, asked about their homes. A bell started ringing. We said goodbye.

'Remember this day, Ruskin,' said my father.

He patted me gently on the head and walked away.

I never saw him again.

Three months later I heard that he had passed away in the military hospital in Calcutta.

I dream of him sometimes, and in my dream he is always the same, caring for me and leading me by the hand along old familiar roads.

And of course I remember that day. Over sixty-five years have passed, but it's as fresh as yesterday.

lonely or alone?

Death moves about at random, without discriminating between the innocent and the evil, the poor and the rich. The only difference is that the poor usually handle it better.

I heard today that the peanut vendor had died. The old man would always be in the dark, windy corner in Landour Bazaar, hunched up over the charcoal fire on which he roasted his peanuts. He'd been there for as long as I could remember, and he could be seen at almost any hour of the day or night. Summer or winter, he stayed close to his fire.

He was probably quite tall, but I never saw him standing up. One judged his height from his long, loose limbs. He was very thin, and the high cheekbones added to the tautness of his tightly stretched skin.

His peanuts were always fresh, crisp and hot. They were popular with the small boys who had a few coins to spend on their way to and from school, and with the patrons of the cinemas, many of whom made straight for the windy corner during intervals or when the show was over. On cold winter evenings, or misty monsoon days, there was always a demand for the old man's peanuts.

No one knew his name. No one had ever thought of asking him for it. One just took him for granted. He was as fixed a landmark as the clock tower or the old cherry tree that grows crookedly from the hillside. The tree was always being lopped; the clock often stopped. The peanut vendor seemed less perishable than the tree, more dependable than the clock. He had no family, but in a way all the world was his family, because he was in continuous contact with people. And yet he was a remote sort of being; always polite, even to children, but never familiar. There is a distinction to be made between aloneness and loneliness. The peanut vendor was seldom alone; but he must have been lonely.

On summer nights he rolled himself up in a thin blanket and slept on the ground, beside the dying embers of his fire. During the winter, he waited until the last show was over, before retiring to the coolies' shed where there was some protection from the biting wind.

Did he enjoy being alive? I wonder now. He was not a joyful person; but then, neither was he miserable. I should think he was a genuine stoic, one of those who do not attach overmuch importance to themselves, who are emotionally uninvolved, content with their limitations, their dark corners. I wanted to get to know the old man better, to sound him out on the immense questions involved in roasting peanuts all his life; but it's too late now. Today his dark corner was deserted; the old man had vanished; the coolies had carried him down to the cremation ground.

'He died in his sleep,' said the tea-shop owner. 'He was very old.'

Very old. Sufficient reason to die.

But that corner is very empty, very dark, and I know that whenever I pass it I will be haunted by visions of the old peanut vendor, troubled by the questions I failed to ask.

a mountain stream

There is a brook at the bottom of the hill. From where I live I can always hear its murmur, but I am no longer conscious of the sound except when I return from a trip to the plains.

And yet I have grown so used to the constant music of water that when I leave it behind I feel naked and alone, bereft of my moorings. It is like getting accustomed to the friendly rattle of teacups every morning, and then waking one day to a deathly stillness and a fleeting moment of panic.

Below the house is a forest of oak and maple and

rhododendron. A path twists its way down through
the trees over an open ridge where red sorrel grows
wild and then down steeply through a tangle of
thorn bushes, creepers and rangal-bamboo.

At the bottom of the hill the path leads on to a
grassy verge, surrounded by wild rose. The stream
runs close by the verge, tumbling over smooth pebbles
over rocks worn yellow with age on its way to the
plains and to the little Song river and finally to the
sacred Ganga.

When I first discovered the stream it was April and
the wild roses were flowering, small white blossoms
lying in clusters. There were still pink and blue
primroses on the hill slopes and an occasional late-
flowering rhododendron provided a splash of red
against the dark green of the hill.

A spotted forktail, a bird of the Himalayan streams,
was much in evidence during those early visits. It
moved nimbly over the boulders with a fairy tread
and continually wagged its tail. Both of us had a
fondness for standing in running water. Once, while
I stood in the stream. I saw a snake swim past, a slim
brown snake, beautiful and lonely. A snake in water
is a lovely creature.

In May and June, when the hills are always brown
and dry, it remained cool and green near the stream

where ferns and maidenhair and long grasses continued to thrive. Downstream, I found a small pool where I could bathe and a cave with water dripping from the roof, the water spangled gold and silver in the shafts of sunlight that pushed through the slits in the cave-roof.

Few people came here. Sometimes a milkman or a coalburner would cross the stream on his way to a village; but, the nearby hill station's summer visitors had not discovered this haven of wild and green things.

The monkeys—langurs with white and silver-grey fur, black faces and long swishing tails—had discovered the place but they kept to the trees and sunlit slopes. They grew quite accustomed to my presence and carried on about their work and play as though I did not exist.

The young ones scuffled and wrestled like boys while their parents attended to each others toilettes, stretching themselves out on the grass, beautiful animals with slim waists and long sinewy legs and tails full of character. They were clean and polite, much nicer than the red monkeys of the plains.

During the rains the stream became a rushing torrent, bushes and small trees were swept away and the friendly murmur of the water became a threatening boom. I did not visit the place too often. There were leeches in the long grass and they would fasten themselves onto my legs and feast on my blood.

But it was always worthwhile tramping through the forest to feast my eyes on the foliage that sprang up in tropical profusion—soft, spongy moss; great staghorn fern on the trunks of trees; mysterious and sometimes evil-looking lilies and orchids, wild dahlias and the climbing convolvulus opening its purple secrets to the morning sun.

And when the rains were over and it was October and the birds were in song again, I could lie in the sun on sweet-smelling grass and gaze up through a pattern of oak leaves into a blind-blue heaven. And I would thank my God for leaves and grass and the smell of things. The smell of mint and myrtle and bruised clover, and the touch of things, the touch of grass and air and sky, the touch of the sky's blueness.

And then after a November hail-storm it was winter and I could not lie on the frostbitten grass. The sound of the stream was the same but I missed the birds; and the grey skies came clutching at my heart and the rain and sleet drove me indoors.

It snowed—the snow lay heavy on the branches of the oak trees and piled up in the culverts—and the grass and the ferns and wild flowers were pressed to sleep beneath a cold white blanket, but the stream flowed on, pushing its way through and under the whiteness, towards another river, towards another spring.

a lime tree in the hills

I wake to what sounds like the din of a factory buzzer but is in fact the music of a single vociferous cicada in the lime tree near my bed.

We have slept out of doors. I wake at first light, focus on a pattern of small, glossy leaves, and then through them see the mountains, the mighty Himalayas, striding away into an immensity of sky.

'In a thousand ages of the gods I could not tell thee of the glories of Himachal.' So a poet confessed at the dawn of Indian history, and no one since has been able to do real justice to the Himalayas. We have climbed their highest peaks, but still the mountains remain remote, mysterious, primeval.

No wonder, then, that the people who live on these mountain slopes, in the mist-filled valleys of Garhwal, have long since beamed humility, patience, and a quiet reserve.

I am their guest for a few days. My friend, Gajadhar, has brought me to his home, to his village above the little Nayar river. We took a train up to the foothills and then we took a bus, and when we were in the hills we walked until we came to this village called Manjari clinging to the terraced slopes of a very proud, very permanent mountain.

It is my fourth morning in the village. Other mornings I was waked by the throaty chuckles of the red-billed blue magpies, but today the cicada has drowned all birdsong.

Early though it is, I am the last to get up. Gajadhar is exercising in the courtyard. He has a fine physique, with the sturdy legs that most Garhwalis possess. I am sure he will realize his ambition of getting into the army. His younger brother, Chakradhar, a slim fair youth, is milking the family's buffalo. Their mother is lighting a fire. She is a handsome woman, although her ears, weighed down by heavy silver earrings, have lost their natural shape. The smaller children, a boy and a girl, are getting ready for school. Their father is in the army, and he is away for most of the year. Gajadhar has been going to a college in the plains; but his mother, with the help of Chakradhar, manages to look after the fields, the house, the goats, and the buffalo. There are spring sowings of corn; monsoon ploughings; September harvestings of rice, and then again autumn sowings of wheat and barley.

They depend on rainfall here, as the village is far above the river. The monsoon is still a month away, but there must be water for cooking, washing, and drinking, and this has to be fetched from the river. And so, after a glass each of hot buffalo's milk, the two brothers and I set off down a rough track to the river.

The sun has climbed the mountains but it has yet to reach the narrow valley. We bathe in the river. Gajadhar and Chakradhar dive in off a massive rock, but I wade in circumspectly, unfamiliar with the river's depth and currents. The water, a milky blue, has come from the melting snows and is very cold. I bathe quickly and then dash for a strip of sand where a little sunshine has now spilt down the mountain in warm, golden pools of light.

A little later, buckets filled, we stroll up the steep mountainside. A different way this time. We have to take the proper path if we are not to come tumbling down with our pails of water. The path leads up past the school, a small temple, and a single shop in which it is possible to buy soap, salt, and a few other necessities. It is also the post office.

The postman has yet to arrive. The mail is brought in relays from Lansdowne, about thirty miles distant. The Manjari postman, who has to cover eight miles and deliver letters at several small villages on the route, should arrive around noon. He also serves as a newspaper, bringing the village people news of the outside world. Over the years he has acquired a reputation for being highly inventive and sometimes creating his own news; so much so that when he told the villagers that men had landed on the moon no one believed him. There are still a few sceptics.

Gajadhar has been walking out of the village almost every day, anxious for a letter. He is expecting the result of his army entrance exam. If he is successful, he will be called for an interview. And then, if he makes a good impression, he will be given training as an officer cadet. After two years he will be a second lieutenant! His father, after twelve years in the army, is only a corporal. But his father never went to school. There were no schools in the hills in those days.

As we pass the small village school, the children, who have been having a break, crowd round us, eager to have a glimpse of me. They have never seen a white face before. The adults had dealt with British officials in the 1940s but it is over twenty years since a European stepped into the village. I am the cynosure of all eyes. The children exclaim, point at me with delight, chatter among themselves. I might be a visitor from another planet instead of just an itinerant writer from the plains.

For Gajadhar, the day is a trial of his patience. First we hear that there has been a landslide and that the postman cannot reach us. Then we hear that, although there was a landslide, the postman had already passed the spot in safety. Another rumour has it that the postman disappeared with the landslide! This is soon denied. The postman is safe. It was only the mailbag that disappeared!

And then, at two in the afternoon, the postman turns up. He tells us that there was indeed a landslide but that it took place on someone else's route. A mischievous urchin who passed him on the way was apparently responsible for all the rumours. But we suspect the postman of having something to do with them.

Yes, Gajadhar has passed his exam and will leave with me in the morning. We have to be up early to complete the thirty-mile trek in a single day. And so, after an evening with friends, and a partridge for dinner (a present from a neighbour who thinks Gajadhar will make a fine husband for his comely daughter), we retire to our beds: I, to my cot under the lime tree. The moon has not yet risen and the cicadas are silent.

I stretch myself out on the cot under a sky brilliant with stars. And as I close my eyes someone brushes against the lime tree, bruising its leaves; and the good fresh fragrance of lime comes to me on the night air, making that moment memorable for all time.

sounds i like to hear

All night the rain has been drumming on the corrugated tin roof. There has been no storm, no thunder just the steady swish of a tropical downpour. It helps one to lie awake; at the same time, it doesn't keep one from sleeping.

It is a good sound to read by—the rain outside, the quiet within—and, although tin roofs are given to springing unaccountable leaks, there is in general a feeling of being untouched by, and yet in touch with, the rain.

Gentle rain on a tin roof is one of my favourite

sounds. And early in the morning, when the rain has stopped, there are other sounds I like to hear—a crow shaking the raindrops from his feathers and cawing rather disconsolately; babblers and bulbuls bustling in and out of bushes and long grass in search of worms and insects; the sweet, ascending trill of the Himalayan whistling-thrush; dogs rushing through damp undergrowth.

A cherry tree, bowed down by the heavy rain, suddenly rights itself, flinging pellets of water in my face.

Some of the best sounds are made by water. The water of a mountain stream, always in a hurry, bubbling over rocks and chattering, 'I'm late, I'm late!' like the White Rabbit, tumbling over itself in its anxiety to reach the bottom of the hill, the sound of the sea, especially when it is far away—or when you hear it by putting a seashell to your ear. The sound made by dry and thirsty earth, as it sucks at a sprinkling of water. Or the sound of a child drinking thirstily the water running down his chin and throat.

Water gushing out of the pans on an old well outside a village while a camel moves silently round the well. Bullock-cart wheels creaking over rough country roads. The clip-clop of a pony carriage, and the tinkle of its bell, and the singsong call of its driver . . .

Bells in the hills. A schoolbell ringing, and children's voices drifting through an open window. A temple-bell, heard faintly from across the valley. Heavy silver ankle-bells on the feet of sturdy hill women. Sheep bells heard high up on the mountainside.

Do falling petals make a sound? Just the tiniest and softest of sounds, like the drift of falling snow. Of course big flowers, like dahlias, drop their petals with a very definite flop. These are showoffs, like the hawk-moth who comes flapping into the rooms at night instead of emulating the butterfly dipping lazily on the afternoon breeze.

One must return to the birds for favourite sounds, and the birds of the plains differ from the birds of the hills. On a cold winter morning in the plains of northern India, if you walk some way into the jungle you will hear the familiar call of the black partridge: *Bhagwan teri qudrat* it seems to cry, which means: 'Oh God! Great is thy might.'

The cry rises from the bushes in all directions; but an hour later not a bird is to be seen or heard and the jungle is so very still that the silence seems to shout at you.

There are sounds that come from a distance, beautiful because they are far away, voices on the wind—they 'walked upon the wings of the wind'. The cries of fishermen out on the river. Drums beating rhythmically in a distant village. The croaking of frogs from the rainwater pond behind the house. I mean frogs at a distance. A frog croaking beneath one's window is as welcome as a motor horn.

But some people like motor horns. I know a taxi-driver who never misses an opportunity to use his horn. It was made to his own specifications, and it gives out a resonant bugle-call. He never tires of using it. Cyclists and pedestrians always scatter at his approach. Other cars veer off the road. He is proud of his horn. He loves its strident sound—which only goes to show that some men's sounds are other men's noises!

Homely sounds, though we don't often think about them, are the ones we miss most when they are gone. A kettle on the boil. A door that creaks on its hinges. Old sofa springs. Familiar voices lighting up the dark. Ducks quacking in the rain.

And so we return to the rain, with which my favourite sounds began.

I have sat out in the open at night, after a shower of rain when the whole air is murmuring and tinkling with the voices of crickets and grasshoppers and little frogs. There is one melodious sound, a swift repeated trill, which I have never been able to trace to its source. Perhaps it is a little tree frog. Or it may be a small green cricket. I shall never know.

I am not sure that I really want to know. In an age when a scientific and rational explanation has been given for almost everything we see and touch and hear, it is good to be left with one small mystery, a mystery sweet and satisfying and entirely my own.

catch a moonbeam

I have lived with these two windows for twenty-five years, and I haven't tired of them. The view hasn't changed, but the cloud patterns are never the same, the bird-song varies, so does the blue dome of the sky, which at night is like a tent of deep purple spangled all over. Some nights are dark, lit up only by glow-worms or fireflies. Other nights are bright, with the full moon coming up over the crest of the mountain and sending a moonbeam in at my window, over my bed and then across my desk to light up the face of the little laughing Buddha who reposes there.

He seems more amused than ever in the light of the moon; laughing tolerantly at the foibles of the human race and mine in particular.

Yes, I've spent twenty-five years in this room and I haven't tired of it as yet, in spite of the attentions of monkeys, mice, moths, spiders and beetles. Recently, a shrew (a *chuchundar*) has taken up residence in a bookshelf. He comes out at night, squeaking and blundering about; apparently they don't see too well.

'Don't kill it,' says Gautam. '*Chuchundars* are lucky. It will bring you money.'

No wonder there was a cheque in the mail from one of my publishers.

The only thing that sometimes troubles me at night is the wind. It can be very fierce. It has blown the roof off a couple of times and knocked down a spruce tree just above the house. These cyclonic winds can make a lot of noise and last for a day or two before moving on. I have always enjoyed reading about strong winds and stormy weather—Conrad's *Typhoon*, Nordhoff and Hall's *Hurricane*, Richard Hughes' *High Wind in Jamaica*—but in reality I prefer the gentle zephyr of a summer's day.

And yet, I have identified with the wind in more than one attempt at verse. Back in my Maplewood days, little Rakesh, then two or three, had been taken back to his village by his parents. I had grown attached to the little fellow, the house was empty without him, and I missed our little walks and romps in the garden. And I wrote this poem:

I was the wind last night—
I vaulted the mountains and crossed seven rivers.
And turned aside the tall trees guarding the valley.
I caught glimpses of you through the window.
As I wandered around the little stone house.
They would not let me in; too cold a wind!
I hung around listlessly, afraid to call too loud.
Then like a weary man limped homewards over
*   the sleeping mountains.*
When will I learn the secret of stillness?

And now, thirty years on, I think I have learnt something of the value of stillness. I don't fret so much; I laugh at myself more often; I don't laugh at others, I live life at my own pace.

Is this wisdom, or is it just old age?

a year with suzie

Suzie came into my life when she was just three weeks old—really too small a baby to be adopted by an inexperienced bachelor. Perhaps I should make it clear at the start that Suzie is a Siamese cat.

I had told a friend that I needed a pet to share my rather lonely life on the outskirts of a north Indian hill station. I had expected to receive a dog; but when the kitten arrived, its small questing head with the chocolate-tipped ears thrust out of a friend's coat pocket, I fell in love at first sight. And, taking its sex for granted, I named the kitten Suzie.

Suzie spent her first night curled up in a tea cosy. She showed her good breeding right from the start by selecting a commodious pot of geraniums for her morning ablutions. A puppy, I reflected, would have been less discriminating.

Like most Siamese cats, she showed a dislike for milk; and I was faced with the problem of obtaining a regular supply of meat. As I lived two miles from the nearest butcher, I took meat only once or twice a week; but Suzie disdained a vegetarian diet. I solved the problem by purchasing a month's supply of tinned sardines and feeding her exclusively on fish. She liked butter too, and used it to polish her coat. All this proved expensive, but I was hoping that as she grew older her natural instincts would result in her bringing in her own supplies.

I was not disappointed. She was barely a month old when she snapped up a large moth that flew in through the open windows on a balmy September night. With all the savage artistry of her species, Suzie dissected this choice morsel and devoured it with relish. A few days later I found, on the kitchen floor, the head and tail of a mouse. The bright innocence of Suzie's sky-blue eyes told me where the rest of the mouse was now lodged.

Cats rarely answer to their names; but Suzie often

does. Moreover, I had tied a little bell to her neck, and this generally tells me where she is. Her favourite haunt is a cherry tree. When a pair of thrushes were building a nest, Suzie learnt to climb this tree beautifully—and the birds went elsewhere. There is truth in the saying that the cat is the aunt of the tiger, and taught the tiger everything except how to climb a tree.

If a cat and a dog are properly introduced to each other, they make the best of friends. It did not take Suzie long to develop a playful, nose-tapping relationship with my neighbour's Peke. Another dog, a rather doleful, good-natured Cocker, permitted Suzie to sleep beneath her on cold days. Such was Suzie's charm that she was soon being fed by my neighbours, and this generosity solved my food problems. People took pity on us. Bachelors and kittens are suitable objects for compassion.

Suzie must have been about five months old when I discovered, to my dismay and embarrassment, that my cat was really a male. But I scorned all suggestions for a change of name: he had been Suzie from his infancy, and he would keep his girl's name for the rest of his time with me.

I had been warned that as soon as Suzie was eight months old he would start staying out late at nights, or even remaining away for several days in his search for a suitable mate. But Suzie was not like other males. He stayed at home, and the queens came to him. There was a beautiful black creature with yellow eyes, straight out of Edgar Allan Poe, and a handsome wild cat from the forest, who came to the front door on alternate nights (never together). Suzie would go out and meet his admirers, and frolic with them in the long, dew-drenched monsoon grass, before returning indoors to sleep deeply and sweetly at the foot of my bed.

Suzie likes people. I think he finds them comfortable. If there are guests, he will always choose the one with the broadest, most accommodating lap. At night he usually sleeps on my tummy (he likes its rise and fall, as I breathe) and if it gets cold, he curls up in the hollow behind my knees.

In the house, during the day, he is unobtrusive. Outside, he has his own pursuits and pleasures, whether it be stalking garden lizards or too familiar myna birds and crows. Sometimes I find him curled up on my typewriter, reminding me that I have not been working regularly of late. He likes music (or is it just the vibrations from the set?) and a favourite spot of his, ever since childhood, has been beside the radio.

At the time of writing Suzie is in the garden, among the marigolds. I doubt if he will find any lizards there. But perhaps this time he is only looking for fairies.

the charm of elephants

Everyone likes elephants. Go where you will, you won't hear a harsh word against these outsize animals, who combine power with gentleness, a childish sulkiness with good humour, and great girth with a ballet-dancer's poise.

Dickens wrote that the elephant employed the worst tailor in the world, but Dickens wasn't a poet. 'An eye like the antelope's, a waist like the lion's, and a gait like the elephant's—these, according to an ancient Indian sage, were the outstanding characteristics of ideal femininity.

The elephant is a firm favourite in Hindu and Buddhist folklore, and in India there is a god called Ganesh who has an elephant's head. How he got his head is rather a long story, but Ganesh is the god of good beginnings. The businessman who opens a new ledger, the writers who starts a new book, and the traveller about to set out on a journey, all invoke the blessings of Ganesh.

Elephants are not sacred, like cows, but they are held in great affection, and no animal has names as pretty as those given to an elephant by his *mahout*, or keeper. Necklace of Beauty, Lily, Rose, Jasmine, Lotus, Garland of Marigolds, Silver Star, Black Snake and Golden One: these are only a few of the names elephants receive.

But why are these animals held in such great esteem?

The reasons are not hard to fine. Elephants are intelligent, hard-working and obedient. They like men, and adjust themselves quickly to the ways of men (I am alluding to the Indian, and not the African elephant; the latter's fine ivory tusks have made him a hunted, tragic creature). Elephants return affection, they are nimble and strong, and they are wonderful to look at.

I don't think you will find elephants in the streets

of Nairobi, but you will frequently see them in the streets of Delhi or Colombo or Rangoon. They are patient with traffic, and co-exist wonderfully well with buses, cars, horse-drawn buggies, cyclists and bullock carts.

Though there are still many wild elephants in India, they can almost be classified as domestic animals, for they feel quite at home with human beings. Wild elephants are usually rounded up by tame elephants, who exert an immediate civilizing effect on their brethren! But elephants can be unpredictable. I have seen a tame elephant rescue marooned villagers from an island in the middle of a flooded river; yet on another occasion this same elephant went berserk and smashed up the village post office.

Elephants are noted for their nimbleness, and in parts of Assam there is a belief that wild elephants sometimes assemble together to dance. A *mahout* once told me that he had come upon a large forest clearing, the floor beaten smooth and hard. 'It was an elephant *nautch-khana*,' he said. A ballroom!

While there is nothing to substantiate this story, it is true that elephants (like stout people, who are often light dancers) are very buoyant on both land and water. There is no reason why they shouldn't dance, and I am quite happy to go along with the quaint belief that elephants meet by moonlight in their forest ballrooms to dance their reels and quadrilles. The music they produce with their trunks is no better or worse than the music of a bagpipe.

'There are many footsteps in the footprint of an elephant,' is an old Indian saying—for in former times it was only rajas who could afford to keep their own elephants, and rajas had large retinues. In old forts and palaces throughout India there are special elephant paths and high-arched elephant-gates, through which the State elephants once marched.

On ceremonial occasions an elephant is still 'dressed'. He is made to lie down by his *mahout* and then he is washed like a child, raising his head or leg at a word, while the *mahout*'s small son climbs about the animal's huge bulk and scrubs him with a brick. The elephant sometimes plays with the soapy water, blowing clouds of vapour from his trunk.

When the washing is over, he is dressed. First the forehead, trunk and ears are painted in bold patterns; there are *mahouts* who are very skilful in this work. Then the howdah is girt on with cotton ropes, which do not chafe the skin. The howdah, too, is lavishly decorated, sometimes with gold and silver ornaments.

The elephant goes through all this with great

patience, but sometimes, when all is ready, he will suddenly fling a bunch of leaves and fodder over his back, to give his *mahout* a little extra work before the parade begins.

At one time elephants were taken by ship from Calcutta to Chittagong, down on the Bay of Bengal. They were needed in Chittagong to help in piling timber, a job which they performed with neatness and precision.

A steamer with forty elephants aboard sailed down the Hooghly, anchoring for the night in a calm sea off Saugor Island. The ship's transport officer did not know that elephants are among the most restless creatures alive, always in motion. At first the crew said it was a ground swell that made the ship roll so much, but they soon found that it was due to the movements of the elephants.

The great beasts had discovered that by swaying to and fro, all together, they could produce a pleasing rhythmic motion. So, they rolled and swung in unison, till the ship was in danger of rolling over with them.

The *mahouts* were hurried down into the hold, and, each seated on an elephant, made the creatures break step. The swaying of the ship ceased; but another difficulty was encountered in carrying fodder down the narrow passageway between the elephants.

They would allow a laden coolie to proceed some way, and then one of their number, quietly mischievous, would trip the man over with its trunk, while the others snatched away the bundles of grass. Finally the coolies had to crawl over the backs of the elephants to get to the far end of the hold.

When the ship arrived in port there was no wharf, and the animals had to swim and wade through a mile of water from the anchorage to the shore. The first elephant was lowered from the deck to the water, with his *mahout* on his neck, and a Lascar seaman clinging to the chain to let go the swivel. The man let go too soon, the elephant fell with a mighty splash, while the suddenly released chain shot the astonished seaman like a bolt from a catapult into the sea some fifty yards away.

But no one came to any harm, and the elephants made their way safely ashore. To anyone who may have been standing on the shore it must have been a most unusual and awe-inspiring sight, as those forty great elephants rose out of the sea, like monsters of the deep, to walk majestically through the surf towards new forests and a new life.

trees from a window

If I open the window and jump, I should land quite safely in the branches of a Himalayan oak. The incline of the hill is such that my first-floor window opens on to what must, I suppose, be the second-floor of the tree.

I have never made the jump, but the big *langoors*—black-faced monkeys with long, swishing tails, who sometimes visit this forest—have often leapt from the trees on to the corrugated tin roof of the old cottage, and made a noise fit to wake the bats sleeping in the recess between roof and ceiling.

The cottage was built at the turn of the last century by an English family who used the granite rocks found in the Mussoorie hills. It is still a reliable shelter in monsoon rain or winter storm, but the tin roof rusts quickly and needs constant attention if it is not to let in wind, rain, dust and insects. Still, the house was not built for this age, and the noise of a passing jet makes the whole building quiver to its foundations.

The big window in the sitting-room is the best part of the cottage. The trees outside are almost within one's reach. The nearest is a walnut tree—only one, but it gives us a basket of walnuts every September.

The hill people have an old belief (which I think has a parallel in England) that the kernel of the walnut, because it is shaped rather like the human brain, is a cure for disorders of the mind.

The flower of the rhododendron is also credited with curative properties, but I am not sure just what it is supposed to cure. The hill people make a pleasant jam from the flowers, and I have seen a party of noisy black bulbuls getting drunk by imbibing too much of the nectar. The flowers are in bloom in March, and are like tongues of fire leaping out of the dark forest.

Most of the forest consists of oak and deodar. The

Himalayan deodar is the same tree as the cedar of Lebanon. Its name is derived from the Sanskrit *devdar*, which means tree of God. And having lived with deodars, I can understand God having a favourite among trees.

It is easily the most noble tree of the Himalayas. It has dignity, grace and strength. Watch it shrug the snow off its shoulders with a gentle disdain and you will get an idea of its dignity. Watch it catch the wind and make it sing, sadly and softly, in its slim green branches, and you will get an idea of its divinity. It is not as fragrant as the pine, but it makes sweeter music.

The oaks (these are not English oaks) are rather stunted and untidy, but they are hospitable to birds and insects. The steady tapping of a woodpecker hunting for his food in the creased and knobbly bark tells us as much. It is a good tree for the privacy of birds, its crooked branches spreading with no particular effect in mind, and sometimes the tree seems uninhabited, until there is a whirring sound, as of a helicopter approaching, and a party of long-tailed blue magpies stream across the forest glade.

There are birds in the trees throughout the year— in February, flocks of spring-green parrots, white-cheeked bulbuls, and sometimes the paradise flycatcher; in summer, the whistling-thrush, often heard but not seen, its song sweet and pure but somehow incomplete, as though, towards the end, it had forgotten the tune; and the barbet, which sits right on top of the tallest deodar and keeps up an interminable chant.

The hillmen have a legend that the barbet is the reincarnation of the soul of a moneylender, who died of grief at the unjust termination of a lawsuit, and that eternally his plaint rises to heaven: '*Un-nee-ow, un-nee-ow,*' which means, 'Injustice, injustice!'

In July and August, when the hawthorn berries are ripe, the tree is visited by green pigeons, who clamber about the fruit-laden twigs upside-down. And during the winter, a redstart perches on the bare branches of the medlar tree and whistles cheerfully. He has come down from higher places, and will winter in the garden.

Open the window at night, and there is usually something to listen to: the shuffle of porcupines emerging for their nocturnal diggings; or the cry of a barking deer which has scented a panther; or the sawing grunt of the panther itself, calling to its mate. Or if you are very lucky you will see the moon coming up over the mountains, and two distant deodars in perfect silhouette.

Occasionally a bat flies in at the window and out again at another. Or a large ungainly bamboo-beetle will blunder in, flop into the water-bowl, be rescued from drowning and ejected into the garden—only to blunder in again a few minutes later.

Some sounds cannot be recognized. They are strange night sounds, the sounds of the tree themselves, stretching their limbs in the dark, shifting a little, flexing their fingers.

They know me well, these trees. They know my face in the window, they see me watching them, watching them grow, and listening to their secrets, bowing my head before their outstretched arms and hoping for their benediction.

monsoon medley

One of my greatest pleasures lies in watching a plant grow—from seed to seedling to green branch or bough, to flower, to fruit. It doesn't have to been an exotic pot-plant, although I've always got on well with geraniums.

In my small sunny room I have a pet tomato and a bean that threatens to challenge Jack's beanstalk and reach the ceiling. No giant lives in it, unless you count the delicate-limbed praying-mantis that arrived out of the blue and took up residence for a few days. I don't care to have too many insects sharing my living space—but some bettles can be very colourful and I don't mind having them around. There was this bright little emerald creature sitting on my desk the other day; a living jewel, transcending any precious stone that you might find in a ring or bracelet.

This is mid-monsoon, and there are shades of green stretching across my field of vision. The light green of new grass, the dark green of the oaks. Ferns festooned on the trunks of the trees. The little purple flowers of the wood-sorrel opening in the morning light. The balsam grows rampant. The ground orchids infiltrate the hillside. And watch out for the nettles!

All is green, except when the mist descends or rather, climbs up from the valley to cling to the hillsides. Then all is a glossy whiteness. Only briefly does the sky open to give us a glimpse of blue.

The geraniums could do with a little sunshine. They will have to wait a few weeks.

Rajveer Handa saw a leopard a few nights ago. He was sitting in his front room when he heard his dog bark outside. There was the sound of a scuffle. He got up, seized his walnut-wood walking-stick and opened the front door. The leopard was astride the struggling dog. Rajveer gave it a blow on the head. It released the dog and hounded away.

Rajveer brought the dog inside and locked all

doors and windows. A little later, when he was about to go to bed, he looked out of the front window. The leopard was stretched out on the grass, its gaze fixed expectantly on the front door. Maybe the dog would emerge again! Yes, even leopards live on hope ...

The street dogs wander about all night without being taken. But then, there's not much meat on them. They survive by virtue of their emaciated condition. Mr Spots would much prefer a well-fed pet dog.

to see a tiger

Mr Kishore drove me out to the forest rest house in his jeep, told me he'd be back in two days, and left me in the jungle. The caretaker of the rest house, a retired Indian Army corporal, made me a cup of tea.

'You have come to see the animals, sir?'

'Yes,' I said, looking around the clearing in front of the house, where a few domestic fowls scrabbled in the dust. 'Will I have to go far?'

'This is the best place, sir,' said the caretaker. 'See, the river is just below.'

A stream of clear mountain water ran through a

shady glade of sal and shisham trees about fifty yards from the house.

'The animals come at night,' said the caretaker. 'You can sit in the verandah, with a cup of tea, and watch them. You must be very quiet, of course.'

'Will I see a tiger?' I asked. 'I've come to see a tiger.'

'Perhaps the tiger will come, sir,' said the caretaker with a tolerant smile. 'He will do his best, I am sure.'

He made me a simple lunch of rice and lentils, flavoured with a mango pickle. I spent the afternoon with a book taken from the rest house bookshelf. The small library hadn't been touched for over twenty years, and I had to make my choice from Marie Corelli, P.C. Wren, and early Wodehouse. I plumped for a Wodehouse—*Love Among the Chickens*. A peacock flaunted its tail feathers on the lawn, but I was not distracted. I had seen plenty of peacocks.

When it grew dark, I took up my position in the verandah, on an old cane chair. Bhag Singh, the caretaker, brought me dinner on a brass *thali* (tray), with two different vegetables in separate *katoris* (brass bowls). The chapaties came in relays, brought hot from the kitchen by Bhag Singh's ten-year-old son. Then, sustained by more tea, sweet and milky, I began my vigil. It took an hour for Bhag Singh's

family to settle down for the night in their outhouse.
Their pi-dog stood outside, barking at me for half an
hour, before he too fell asleep. The moon came up
over the foothills, and the stream could be seen quite
clearly.

And then a strange sound filled the night air. Not
the roar of a tiger, nor the sawing of a leopard, but
a rising crescendo of noise—*wurk, wurk, wurk*—
issuing from the muddy banks near the stream. All
the frogs in the jungle seemed to have gathered there
that night. They must have been having a sort of Old
Boys' Reunion, because everyone seemed to have
something to say for himself. The speeches continued
for about an hour. Then the meeting broke up, and
silence returned to the forest.

A jackal slunk across the clearing. A puff of wind
brushed through the trees. I was almost asleep when
a cicada burst into violent music in a nearby tree. I
started, and stared out at the silver, moon-green
stream; but no animals came to drink that night.

The next evening Bhag Singh offered to sit up with
me. He placed a charcoal-burner on the verandah,
and topped it with a large basin of tea.

'Whenever you feel sleepy, sir, I'll give you a glass
of tea.'

Did we hear a panther—or was it someone sawing

wood? The sounds are similar, in the distance. The frogs started up again. The Old Boys must have brought their wives along this time, because instead of speeches there was general conversation, exactly like the natter of a cocktail party.

By morning I had drunk over fifteen cups of tea. Out of respect for my grandfather, a pioneer tea-planter in India, I did not complain. Bhag Singh made me an English breakfast—toast, fried eggs, and more tea.

The third night passed in much the same way, except that Bhag Singh's son stayed up with us and drank his quota of tea.

In the morning, Mr Kishore came for me in his jeep. 'Did you see anything?'

'A jackal,' I said.

'Never mind, you'll have better luck next time. Of course, the jungles aren't what they used to be . . .'

I said goodbye to Bhag Singh, and got into the jeep.

We had gone barely a hundred yards along the forest road when Mr Kishore brought the jeep to a sudden, jolting halt.

Right in the middle of the road, about thirty yards in front of us, stood a magnificent full-grown tiger.

The tiger didn't roar. He didn't even snarl. But he gave us what appeared to be a quick, disdainful glance, and then walked majestically across the road and into the jungle.

'What luck!' exclaimed Mr Kishore. 'You can't complain now, can you? You've seen your tiger!'

'Yes,' I said. 'three sleepless nights, and I've seen it—in broad daylight!'

'Never mind,' said Mr Kishore. 'If you're tired, I know just the thing for you—a nice cup of tea!'

I think it was Malcolm Muggeridge who said that the only real Englishmen left in the world were to be found in India.

a pocketful of thoughts

You don't see them so often now, those tiny books and almanacs—genuine pocket books—once so popular with our parents and grandparents; much smaller than the average paperback, often smaller than the palm of the hand. With the advent of coffee-table books, new books keep growing bigger and bigger, rivalling tombstones. And one day, like Alice after drinking from the wrong bottle, they will reach the ceiling and won't have anywhere else to go. The average publisher, who apparently believes that large profits are linked to large books, must look upon these old miniatures with amusement or scorn. They were not meant for coffee-tables, true. They were meant for true booklovers and readers, for they took up very little space—you could slip them into your pocket without any discomfort, either to you or to the pocket.

I have a small collection of these little books, treasured over the years. Foremost is my father's prayer-book, and psalter, with his name, 'Aubrey Bond, Lovedale, 1917', inscribed on the inside back cover. Lovedale is a school in the Nilgiri Hills in south India, where, as a young man, he did his teacher training. He gave it to me soon after I went to a boarding-school in Simla in 1944, and my own name is inscribed on it in his beautiful handwriting.

Another beautiful little prayer book in my collection is called *The Finger Prayer Book*. Bound in soft leather, it is about the same length and breadth as the average middle finger. Replete with psalms, it is the complete *Book of Common Prayer* and not an abridgement; a marvel of miniature book production.

Not much larger is a delicate item in calf-leather, *The Humour of Charles Lamb*. It fits into my wallet and often stays there. It has a tiny portrait of the great essayist followed by some thirty to forty extracts from his essays, such as this favourite of mine: 'Every dead man must take upon himself to be lecturing me with his odious truism, that "Such as he is now, I must shortly be." Not so shortly, friend, perhaps as thou imaginest. In the meantime I am alive. I move about. I am worth twenty of these. Know they betters!'

No fatalist, Lamb. He made no compromise with Father Time. He affirmed that in age we must be as glowing and tempestuous as in youth! And yet Lamb is thought to have been an old-fashioned writer.

Another charming little book is my grandmother's recipe book, small enough to slip into her apron pocket. (You need to be a weightlifter to pick up some of the cookery books that are published today). Its charm lies not so much in its recipes for roast lamb and mint sauce (which are very good too), but because the margins of each page are enlivened with little maxims concerning good food and wise eating. Here are a few pleasing examples:

'There is skill in all things, even in making porridge.'

'Dry bread at home is better than roast meat abroad.'

'Eating and drinking should not keep men from thinking.'

'Light suppers make long lives.'

'Let not your tongue cut your throat!'

Another favourite among my 'little' books is

The Pocket Trivet, An Anthology for Optimists, published by *The Morning Post* newspaper in 1932. But what is a trivet? the unenlightened may well ask. Well, it's a stand for a small pot or kettle, fixed securely over a grate. To be 'right as a trivet' is to be perfectly right—just right, like the short sayings in this book, which is further enlivened by a number of charming woodcuts based on seventeenth-century originals; such as the illustration of a moth hovering over a candle flame and below it the legend: 'I seeke mine owne hurt.'

But the sayings are mostly of a cheering nature, such as Emerson's 'Hitch your wagon to a star!' or the West Indian proverb: 'Every day no Christmas, an' every day no rainy day.'

My book of trivets is a happy example of much concentrated wisdom being collected in a small space—the beauty separated from the dross. It helps me to forget the dilapidated building in which I live and to look instead at the ever-changing cloud patterns as seen from my bedroom window. There is no end to the shapes made by the clouds, or to the stories they set off in my head. We don't have to circle the world in order to find beauty and fulfilment.

After all, most of living has to happen in the mind. And, to quote one anonymous sage from my trivet: 'The world is only the size of each man's head.'

a book lover's lifelong hunt

My mother and stepfather were not great readers, and books were a scarce commodity in my life until I was about twelve. In those lonely childhood years, I was to discover that books could be good friends, steadfast and reliable, and I seized upon almost any printed matter that came my way, whether it was a girls' classic like *Little Women*, or a *True Detective* magazine, or Edgar Allan Poe, or *Insect Life in Mozambique*.

Fifty years on, my reading habits are still as wide-ranging and omnivorous.

But I think it all began in that forest rest house in the Siwalik Hills, a subtropical range cradling the Doon valley in northern India. Here my stepfather and his gun-toting friends were given to hunting the wild animals that still roamed those forests. He was a poor shot, so he cannot really be blamed for the absence of wildlife today; but he did his best to shoot down everything in sight!

On one of these 'shikar' trips, we were staying in a rest house near the Timli Pass. My stepfather and his friends were 'after tiger', and set out every morning with an army of villagers to 'beat' the jungle, in order to drive the tiger out into the open. Never excited by this form of sport, I stayed behind in the rest house, fully expecting complete boredom for the duration of our stay. Exploring the old rest house, I discovered that one of the rooms was furnished with a dusty bookshelf, stacked high with books that hadn't been touched for years.

It was here that I discovered *Three Men in a Boat*, by Jerome K. Jerome, which I finished reading that same day. The next day I read most of the stories in M.R. James's *Ghost Stories of an Antiquary*. On the third day, while the sportsmen were still looking for their tiger, I chuckled over my first Wodehouse (*Love Among the Chickens*), sampled O. Henry, and started on *David Copperfield*. Camp broke up before I could get through *Copperfield*, but the forest ranger said I could keep it, which I did, thus becoming the only person with a trophy to show for the hunt, the clever tiger having proved elusive.

After that adventure, I was always looking for books in unlikely places; and I had knack of finding them, too.

A couple of years ago, I was rummaging through some discarded books at a school jumble sale, when I found a first edition of *Three Men in a Boat*. As this book had been one of my first loves, I felt that my reading adventures had come full cycle. When I think of all the great books I have read over the years, I realize that they have more than made up for the disappointments that sometimes came my way, and that I am indeed a fortunate man. I am sure that other compulsive readers feel the same way.

Although I never went to college, I think I have read as much, if not more, than most college men, so that it would be true to say that I received my education in the second-hand bookshops. London had many, and Calcutta once had a number of them, but I think the prize must go to a small town in Wales called Hay-on-Wye, which has twenty-six bookshops and over 1 million books. It's in the world's quieter corners that book lovers still flourish as a race.

Unlikely, out-of-the-way places often yield up treasures—like the trunkful thrown out of a hotel storeroom, providing me with *The Complete Plays of J.M. Barrie*. Am I the only person around who still reads Barrie? His occasional sentimentality is a sin in the eyes of modern critics, but I must confess to an unabashed enjoyment of plays such as *Mary Rose, Dear Brutus, A Kiss For Cinderella*, and, of course, *Peter Pan*.

I love discovering forgotten or neglected gems which I feel deserve to be read again. One of them was an exquisite essay by the Boston writer, Louise Imogen Guiney (1861–1920), called 'The Precept of Peace', which appeared in her book *Patrins* (1897). A lovely and profound piece of writing, it is typical of the humorous tranquillity with which she faced the failure (financially speaking) of all her books.

Another gem, *Sweet Rocket* (1920), by Mary Johnston, was also a financial failure. It had only the thinnest outline of a story, but she set out her ideas in lyrical prose that seduces the sympathetic reader at every turn of the page. Miss Johnston was a Virginian. She did not travel outside America. But her little book did. I found it buried under a pile of railway timetables at a railway bookstall in Simla, the old summer capital of India—almost as though it had been waiting there for me, these seventy years!

fragrance to the air

I would be the last person to belittle a flower for its lack of fragrance, because there are many spectacular blooms such as the dahlia and the gladioli which have hardly any scent and yet make up for it with their colour and appearance. But it does happen that my own favourite flowers are those with a distinctive fragrance and these are the flowers I would have around me.

The rose, of course, is the world's favourite, a joy to all—even to babies, who enjoy taking them apart, petal by petal. But there are other, less spectacular, less celebrated blooms which have a lovely, sometimes elusive fragrance all their own.

I have a special fondness for antirrhinums—or snapdragons, as they are more commonly known. If I sniff hard at them, I don't catch any scent at all. They seem to hold it back from me. But if I walk past a bed of snapdragons, or even a single plant, the gentlest of fragrance is wafted towards me. If I stop and try to take it all in, it has gone again! I find this quite tantalizing, but it has given me a special regard for this modest flower.

Another humble, even old-fashioned flower, is the wallflower which obviously takes its name from the fact that it thrives on walls. I have seen wallflowers adorn a garden wall in an extravagant and delightful manner, making it a mountain of perfume. They are best grown so as to form dense masses which become literally solid with fiery flowers—blood-red, purple, yellow, orange or bronze, all sending a heady fragrance into the surrounding air.

Carnations, with their strong scent of cloves, are great showoffs. In India, the jasmine and the magnolia are both rather heady and overpowering. The honeysuckle too insists on making its presence known. A honeysuckle creeper flourished outside the window of my room in Mussoorie, and all through the summer its sweet, rather cloying fragrance drifted in through the open window. It was delightful at times, but at other times I had to close the window just so that I could give my attention to other, less intrusive smells—like the soft, sweet scent of petunias (another of my favourites) growing near the doorstep, and great bunches of sweet peas stacked in a bowl on my desk.

It is much the same with chrysanthemums and geraniums. The lemon geranium, for instance, is valued more for its fragrant leaves than for its rather indeterminate blue flowers. And I cannot truthfully say what ordinary mint looks like in flower. The refreshing fragrance of the leaves, when crushed, makes up for any absence of floral display. On the other hand, the multi-coloured loveliness of dahlias is unaccompanied by any scent. Its greenery, when cut or broken, does have a faintly acrid smell, but that's about all.

Not all plants are good to smell. Some leaves, when crushed, will keep strong men at bay! During the monsoon in the plains, neem pods fall and are crushed underfoot, giving out a distinctive odour. Most people dislike the smell, but I find it quite refreshing.

Of course, one man's fragrance might well turn out to be another creature's bad smell. Geraniums, my grandmother insisted, kept snakes away because they couldn't stand the smell of the leaves. She surrounded her bungalow with pots of geraniums. As we never found a snake in the house, she may well have been right. But the evidence is purely circumstantial.

I suppose snakes like some smells, close to the ground, or by now they'd have taken to living in more elevated places. But, turning to a book on reptiles, I learnt from it that in the snake the sense of smell is rather dull. Perhaps it has an aversion to anything that it can smell—such as those aromatic geranium leaves!

Close to Mother Earth, there are many delightful smells, provided you avoid roadsides and freshly manured fields. When I lie on summer grass in some Himalayan meadow, I am conscious of the many good smells around me—the grass itself, redolent of the morning's dew, bruised clover, wild violets, tiny buttercups and golden stars and strawberry flowers and many others I shall never know the names of.

And the earth itself. It smells different in different places. But its loveliest fragrance is known only when it receives a shower of rain. And then the scent of the wet earth rises as though it would give something beautiful back to the clouds. A blend of all the fragrant things that grow upon it.

a bush at hand is good for many a bird

The thing I like most about shrubs and small bushes is that they are about my size or thereabouts. I can meet them on equal terms. Most trees grow tall, they overtake us after a few years, and we find ourselves looking up to them with a certain amount of awe and deference. And so we should.

A bush, on the other hand, may have been in the ground for a long time—thirty or forty years or more—while continuing to remain a bush, man-sizes and approachable. A bush may spread sideways or gain in substance, but it seldom towers over you. This means that I can be on intimate terms with it, know its qualities—of leaf, bud, flower or fruit—and also its inhabitants, be they insects, birds, small mammals, or reptiles.

Of course, we know that bushes are ideal for binding the earth together and preventing erosion. In this respect they are just as important as trees. Every monsoon I witness landslides all about me, but I know the hillside just above my cottage is well knit, knotted and netted, by bilberry and raspberry, wild jasmine, dog rose and bramble, and other shrubs, vines and creepers.

I have made a small bench in the middle of this civilized wilderness. And sitting here, I can look down on my own roof, as well as sideways and upward, into a number of bushes teeming with life throughout the year. This is my favourite place. No one can find me here, unless I call out and make my presence known. The buntings and sparrows grow 'accustomed to my face,' and welcoming the grain I scatter for them, flit about near my feet. One of them, bolder than the rest, alights on my shoe and proceeds to polish his beak on the leather. The sparrows are here all the year round. So are the whistling thrushes, who live in the shadow between the house and the hill, sheltered by a waterwood bush, so called because it likes cold, damp places.

Summer brings the fruit-eating birds, for now the berries are ripe. A pair of green pigeons, rare in these parts, scramble over the branches of a hawthorn bush, delicately picking off the fruit. The raspberry bush is raided by bands of finches and greedy, yellow-bottomed bulbuls. A flock of bright green parrots comes sweeping down on the medlar tree, but they do not stay for long. Taking flight at my approach, they wheel above, green and gold in the sunlight, and make for the plum trees further down the road.

The kingora, a native Himalayan shrub similar to the bilberry, attracts small boys as well as birds. On their way to and from school, the boys scramble up the hillside and help themselves to the small sweet and sour berries. Then, lips stained purple, they go their merry way. The birds return.

Other inhabitants of this shrubland include the skink, a tiny lizard-like reptile, quite harmless. It emerges from its home among stones or roots to sun itself or drink from a leaf-cup of water. I have to protect these skinks from a large prowling tabby cat who thinks the hillside and everything on it belongs to him.

From my bench, I can see him moving stealthily around the corner of my roof. He has his eye on the slow-moving green pigeons. I am sure, I shall have to watch out for him. There wouldn't be much point in encouraging the birds to visit my bushes if the main beneficiary is to be that handsome but single-minded cat.

There are flowering shrubs, too—a tangle of dog-roses, the wild yellow jasmine, a buddleia popular with honey bees, and spreading mayflower which today is covered with small saffron-winged butterflies.

The grass, straw-yellow in winter, is now green and sweet, sprinkled with buttercups and clover. I can abandon the bench and lie on the grass, studying it at close quarters while repeating Whitman's lines:

A child said, 'What is the grass?'
fetching it to me with full hands.
how could I answer the child? I do not
know what it is any more than he.

I am no wiser either, but grass is obviously a good thing, providing a home for crickets and ladybirds and other small creatures. It would not be much fun living on a planet where grass could not grow.

That cat agrees with me. He is flat on his stomach on the grass, inching closer to one of those defenceless little skinks. He has decided that a skink in hand is worth two birds in a bush. I get to my feet, and the skinks run away.

The green pigeons has also flown away. The smaller birds remain where they are; they know they are swift for the prowler. I returned to my bench and the finches and coppersmith arrive and depart.

You might call my shrubbery an arrival and departure lounge for small birds but they are also free to take up residence if they want. Their presence adds stillness to my life. A bush in hand is good for many a bird.

geraniums

I can meditate upon a geranium. That is, I can spend a long time gazing at one.

And while I was gazing at mine, there came a phone call from my accountant informing me that it was time for me to start preparing my income-tax return. And thus, the harsh realities of life intrude upon our poetic fancies—but I shall return to the subject of geraniums at the first opportunity.

And as I can get geraniums to flower in my sunny bedroom, summer and winter, I have every opportunity to do so.

The geranium that has done best is the one I have grown in a large plastic bucket standing on the chest of drawers and facing the early morning sun. Here, protected from wind and rain (both of which are anathema to geraniums), this generous plant has produced no less than eight florets of soft pink confetti. Pastel shades have always appealed to me. And there is something alluring about this sensual pink. Other shades are appealing too—the salmon-pink, the cerise, the flaming red—but this pale pink is restful, intimate. From my bed or desk I can gaze at it and have pleasant thoughts. Is that meditation? Or is it contemplation? The latter, probably. I am really the contemplative type.

But meditation is in fashion—people give and take courses in it!—whereas I have yet to meet someone taking a course in contemplation. I suspect that meditation is something that you do deliberately (hence the need for practise), and contemplation is simply what comes naturally.

When we meditate, we look within, and hopefully there is something to find there. When I look at a flower, I am looking without contemplating at the miracle of creation. I suppose we should do a little of both, just to get the right balance.

ghosts of a peepul tree

The villages of India have always harboured a large variety of ghosts, some of them good, some evil. There are the prets and bhuts, both the spirits of dead men; and the churels, ghosts of women who change their shape after death. Then there is the pisach, a sort of hobgoblin; and the munjia, a mischievous and sometimes sinister evil spirit. They have one thing in common; nearly all of them choose to live in the peepul tree.

There is not much difference between the bhut and the pret: the latter is simply a better class of ghost, less inclined to indulge in malicious activities. It is usually the spirit of one who has loved the earth so m.... that he cannot bear to take final leave of it. The pret lives either in its former home or in a peepul tree, and is something honoured with the title of Purwaj Dev, an ancestor god. Prets often take the form of snakes, living in the garden, where they are fed with milk and honoured by the household.

There is a story of a villager who was in the habit of beating his son unceasingly. One day the villager visited a garden where a Purwaj Dev in the form of a snake was living. The snake threatened to bite and kill the villager unless he promised to give his son better treatment. The villager went away a chastened man. The lady of the house was very fond of the snake and gave it milk every day; and in return for this favour the snake would often guard her baby and rock its cradle.

A ghost which in the past was often responsible for the desertion of a house or even of a village was the churel.

A churel is full of animosity towards men, probably because in life she was unfairly treated by them. She is covered with hair, has the ears of an ape, and her toes are two or three feet in length. Sometimes her feet face backwards. During the day the churel has no power, but at night she lies along the branches of a peepul tree, directly over a footpath. Should any man pass beneath the tree, the churel's prehensile toes stretch out, grip the man by the neck, and throttle him.

The pisach can be a malignant, sometimes amorous ghost. It has no body or shape, but dwells in a peepul tree or a graveyard. In the *Vetal Panchvishi* there is the story of a young wife who, while her husband is in another town, falls in love with a young man. On her husband's return the wife would have nothing to do with him; as soon as he was asleep, she ran to join her lover near the house of her maidservant. But the lover, who had arrived first, was bitten by a cobra, and died before the woman arrived. A pisach (who had seen everything from a nearby peepul tree) now entered the dead man's body, and began to play the lover to the errant wife. After some time, out of sheer wickedness, the pisach bit off the woman's nose, left the corpse, and went back to the peepul tree.

The unfortunate lady, now without a nose, ran home screaming that her husband had bitten it off. The husband was arrested and his execution ordered;

but a stranger suggested that a search might be made at the maidservant's cottage. There they found the lover's body on the bed, and between his teeth was the wife's nose. Finally the husband was acquitted, and the wife placed on a donkey and driven out of the city.

The Mahrattas used to be familiar with an evil spirit known as a munjia.

A munjia is said to be the disembodied spirit of a Brahmin youth who has died before his marriage. Like other spirits, it lives in a peepul tree, often rushing out at tongas, bullock carts and bicycles, and upsetting them. (No instance has as yet been recorded of its trying collisions with a bus.) When passing a peepul tree at night, should anyone be so careless as to yawn without snapping his fingers in front of his mouth, a munjia will dash down his throat and completely ruin him. It is quite possible that people suffering from indigestion have made the mistake of yawning under a peepul tree.

It is not surprising that in villages, after dark, everyone, even the blind, is supposed to carry a lamp. And if you ask the blind man what use a lamp is to him, he will reply: 'Fool, the lamp is not for my benefit, but for yours, lest you stumble against me in the dark.'

solitude

As far as I know, we do not have an anthology on solitude. It's a condition appreciated only by a small minority, I suppose.

It seems to me that most people are scared of solitude, for almost everything is carried out on a crowded scale. Clubs, wedding parties, sporting events, political meetings, victory parades, protests, religious events, *melas*, even prayer meetings—the bigger the crowd, the more successful the event! Let a man be seen walking about the hills or countryside alone, and he will be labelled an eccentric; for to most people loneliness is wrongly linked to unhappiness. Their minds are not deep enough to appreciate the sweetness and balm of solitude; they are afraid of life itself, of coming face to face with themselves.

Most of the time we are taken up with family life or working for a living. To get away from it all, just once in a while, into the hills or fields or bylanes, where 'I am I', is to enjoy undisturbed serenity. It helps one to contemplate, to create a philosophy of life, to take the mind off the nagging cares of pressures of this age of technological mayhem.

Probably the best book on solitude is *Robinson Crusoe*. Crusoe learnt to appreciate and value his enforced solitude. The arrival of Man Friday proved to be rather unsettling, and his subsequent conflict with savage intruders made him even more appreciative of his lost solitude.

Richard Jefferies, in *The Story of My Heart*, claims to be a pagan by nature, and avoids the haunts of men, escaping into the woods with a certain alacrity. He is happiest in the bosom of nature, and is a true solitary, with sun, moon and stars as his companions. An atheist, he does not even seek the companionship of a possible Creator; he simply accepts the natural world as he finds it.

But you do not have to turn your back on the world at large in order to find true solitude. A solitary spirit can move around with the crowd while still holding on to his innate reserve. Take Frobisher, the junior partner in a firm of solicitors in A.E.W. Mason's enjoyable novel, *The House of the Arrow*. 'He was a solitary person. Very few people up till now had mattered to him at all, and even those he could do without. It was his passion to feel that his life and the means of his life did not depend upon the purchased skill of other people ... A half-decked sailing boat which one man could handle, an ice-axe, a rifle, an inexhaustible volume or two like *The Ring and the Book*—these with the stars and his own thoughts had been his companions on many lonely expeditions ...'

Many of Conrad's characters have learnt to live with the solitude of the great oceans—Captain Lingard in *An Outcast of the Islands*, Captain Machheir in *Typhoon*, *Lord Jim*, Conrad himself in *The Secret Sharer*, *The Shadow Line*, and in the character of his narrator, Marlow.

T.E. Lawrence was another who chose the solitary life; indeed, he ended it in complete anonymity; but before that he had captured the solitude of the desert in his great work, *The Seven Pillars of Wisdom*.

solitude

The sea, the desert, the mountains—these under-populated areas of the planet do seem to appeal to the solitary individual, whether writer or adventurer.

Some choose to sail aroud the world in small boats. Others, like Jefferies, remain in their own small patch, yet see the world in a grain of sand.

a postage stamp

I was leafing through an old book, a childhood gift, when a postage stamp slipped out from the pages and on to my hand. Ceylon, 25 c, depicting the Temple of the Tooth, and with King George VI of England peering out at me from the top-right-hand corner. It must have been issued around 1940, at the commencement of World War II. My father had joined the RAF, but whenever he found time he immersed himself in his stamp collection.

How well I remember those stamps albums. There was a trunk full of them. He specialized in Empire stamps, and had some rare issues from Ceylon, India, Burma, Newfoundland, and the islands of the Pacific and the West Indies. He did have a valuable collection, and he said it would be mine some day. While I was with him in Delhi (I was nine at the time) I would help him with the sorting and checking against the catalogue, but he liked to do the mounting himself—very neatly, in specially prepared albums purchased from abroad. His Stanley Gibbons catalogue was like a Bible, constantly referred to for information, values, and help in completing sets. I was encouraged to collect too, and I had my own small album, most of it filled with stamps from Greece. I don't know why I chose Greece—I was probably attracted by the Greek gods and heroes depicted on the stamps—and my father seemed to have an unending supply of Greek stamps which he did not want.

Sometimes he bought stamps, occasionally he sold a few, but the entire collection accompanied him to Calcutta when he was transferred from Delhi in 1943-44. I was placed in a Simla boarding-school. In his last letter to me, written in September of that year, he said that he was looking forward to doing 'stamp work' with me during the winter holidays. But I did not see him again. He died of hepatitis in the British Military hospital. His brother and old mother survived him, and I suppose they disposed of the stamp collection. This rather discouraged me from becoming a collector, but I'll keep this old Ceylon stamp that fell out of a book. It may not have been his; it may not have been mine; but it belongs to that time, and opens the floodgates of memory.

Today, the 29th of July, was my father's birthday (as it is also Siddharth's), and I feel very close to him today, recalling his companionship, giving me all his time when he was free from his duties, introducing me to books, music, films. I have recorded all this elsewhere, but memories were revived, first by the discovery of the old postage stamp, and then by a phone call from Arghia Mukherjee, my friend in Kolkata, who kindly visited my father's grave in the Bhowanipore cemetery—having taken the day off from teaching! He cycled from his home in Howrah to Bhowanipore, a half-hour ride across the Hooghly bridge, getting soaked in the process.

The old Bhowanipore cemetery is one of the better-kept cemeteries in India, partly because it is also a World War II military cemetery, supported by the War Graves Commission.

One of Charles Dickens seven sons, Walter Landor Dickens, was buried here in 1863, but the grave was later removed to the Park Street cemetery, for no good reason. It was part of the Victorian tradition to send boys to India, and Dickens had obtained an East Indian cadetship for Walter Landor (named after the poet Walter Savage Landor). Walter was not a strong boy; he had wanted to be a writer like his father, but was discouraged from this ambition. The climate of India did not agree with him and his health broke down completely. He was invalided home but died (aged twenty-one) as he was passing through Calcutta.

Stamps were not the only things that my father collected. There were several cases of colourful butterflies, most of them caught in the hills around Munnar (in Travancore–Cochin, now Kerala state) where he had spent two or three years as an assistant manager on a tea estate. This was when he was a young man, before he met and married my mother. You have to be young and fairly athletic to chase butterflies up and down the hills. Stamps were easier, more cerebral. As were state crests, postcards, match-box labels.

something to celebrate

Break of day, the early dawn, that's something to celebrate. And most mornings, while it's still dark, I stand at my window until the first light enables me to see the winding roads below, and the distant hills. No, the dawn doesn't come up like thunder, as in Kipling's 'Road to Mandalay'; it approaches softly, quietly, until all is visible—and it's about two hours between first light (roughly 5 a.m. in summer) and actual sunrise (about 7 a.m.), and it's during this period that birds sing, a few people take their 'constitutionals', and one or two vehicles glide past without having to use their horns.

But this morning I thought of something else to celebrate. It's fifty years since my first book was published. And in spite of all indications to the contrary, I have survived—as a writer, as an individual, as a breadwinner, as a lover of beauty.

So many failures and setbacks along the way; but I suppose my inner stubbornness saw me through. 'You're a stubborn little boy,' said Granny when I was six, and she did not intend it as a compliment.

'He's an angel in front of other,' said my mother. 'But a little devil when he's on his own.'

I expect it was the devil in me that made me choose writing as a career in spite of everyone advising against it. 'You'll starve in an attic.' 'You'll never make it—you're not the bestselling type.' 'Write in your spare time—become a school teacher.' 'Join the army, son.' 'Study, and become a Civil Servant. You'll get a pension.'

And so it went on—words of advice from mother, stepfather, aunts and uncles, well-meaning friends and neighbours.

Well, I wasn't afraid to take a job. And then, during my two years in Jersey, Channel Islands, I wrote at night in my aunt's attic room. I sent out stories and articles, all returned through the post with polite rejection slips. My cousins were amused. But my uncle said, 'At least he doesn't give up.'

That was it! That was my mantra. Just three little words: Never give up.

Then three years in London and another dull and dreary office job. The first draft of a novel. Rejected, but words of encouragement from a publisher. Try again. A second draft. Rejected, but why not do it another way? A third draft. They took it!

Back to India, richer by £50. Freelancing from Dehra. Bombarding the Indian newspapers and periodicals with stories and articles. Payments ranged from five to fifty rupees. But most of them did pay. And in 1956 *The Room on the Roof* came out in England, followed by a German translation and a literary prize. A few weeks of fame! But the book did not make any money for my publishers, and they were reluctant to do another. And Indian publishers did not consider fiction in those days. But there were the magazines—at least a dozen that paid. So I wrote a story and a couple of articles every week, and paid my rent and took my meals at a *dhaba* down the road. It wasn't the best of times, but it wasn't the worst of times either, and at twenty-one I could put up with a certain amount of discomfort and indigestion. I was a skinny fellow at the time. I would do my writing at night, by the light of a kerosene lantern, the electricity connection having been cut because of my landlady's inability to pay the bills.

Two years of this, and then to Delhi to seek my fortune. No fortune for me, but a job of sorts, during which time I lived with my mother and stepfather. 'Now, Ruskin, you've a good job, don't give it up.'

But I grew restless. The hills were calling, and Patel Nagar could not compete with them. I wasn't writing much, either. I had to get closer to nature, to forests and mountain streams, and if the words were to come with the old fluency I needed a magic mountain. Not Dehra, which had grown rather seedy, but something higher, more uplifting.

Two years earlier, I'd picked up a copy of *The Story of My Heart* by Richard Jefferies. (It is with me even now.) Here was a writer I could relate to—someone who could not only observe, but who could feel while observing, and to be conscious of his feeling. That was how I wanted to write. The mind requires something higher then prayer, something higher than a god. Like Jefferies, I found that something under the trees, on the hilltops, at sunrise and in the night. In the mountains, there was a deeper meaning everywhere. And if you are sensitive, then you become sensitive to all things, to the least blade of grass, to the dewdrop on the grass.

But I cannot deny that there has always been a

pragmatic side to my nature. If it was only mountain vines and wild violets I would not have been able to sustain my dream of living and writing in the hills. You can't get through life without paying your bills. Sometimes a writer must take on assignments other than those he sets himself.

I was lucky in this regard. I'd been in Mussoorie barely a month when I bumped into young Shakabpa, who'd been at school with me in Simla back in 1950. He was the son of Tibet's finance minister, an important person in the Tibetan heirarchy.

'I've been looking for you,' said Shakabpa. 'Will you help us write a book?'

It turned out that Shakabpa senior was writing a political history of Tibet. He had all the documents at his disposal, but he was dependent on his son's English. Unfortunately Shakabpa junior did not have a very good command of written English. So it was proposed that old Shakabpa would dictate (in Tibetan) to young Shakabpa, who would then give me a fairly literal translation in his English, which I would then transcribe into readable prose.

I went along with the arrangement and spent two hours every morning at the Shakabpas' rented flat on the Mall. They gave me a good retainer, and the work sessions were punctuated by refreshment sessions and the consumption of large quantities of excellent momos. So the work was far from boring. It went on for six months and enabled me to settle into Maplewood Lodge, the cottage I had rented in the woods below Wynbery-Allen School.

A couple of years later Mr Shakabpa's book was published by Yale University. My help was acknowledged in the preliminaries. But I was not looking for a credit line. The assignment had kept me going through a difficult time, and at the end of it I was ready to make another assault on the publishing world with my own stories and belles-lettres.

I was eight years in Maplewood, and two years in Wayside Cottage and during that period I wrote in magazines such as *Blackwood's* in the UK, *The Christian Science Monitor* in Boston, and *The Asian Magazine* in Hong Kong, apart from finding publishers abroad for my early children's-books— *Panther's Moon, Angry River* and *The Blue Umbrella*, stories that are still in print thirty-five years after they were written.

I was also writing for our own papers. In fact, I was busier than I'd ever been in London, Dehradun, or New Delhi. And if I ran out of material I had only to open the window and observe the happenings in the maples and oak trees that grew thickly on the slope below the cottage.

the typewriter

Working at nights in an attic room provided by my aunt, I took six months to complete my first book, a novel. I was eighteen at the time, and though the novel was about growing up in India, I was living in Jersey, in the Channel Islands, earning about £4 a week as a Public Works' clerk.

I hadn't been away from India for as much as a year, but I was very homesick, and writing the book helped to take me back to the people and places I had known and loved.

Working in in the same office was a sympathetic

soul, a senior clerk whose name was Mr Bromley. He came from good Lancashire stock. His wife and son had predeceased him, and he lived alone in lodgings near the St. Helier seafront. As I lived not far away, I would sometimes accompany Mr Bromley home after work, walking with him along the sea wall, watching the waves hissing along the sandy beaches or crashing against the rocks.

I gathered from some of his remarks that he had an incurable disease, and that he had come to live and work in Jersey in the hope that a sunnier climate would help him to get better. He sensed that we were, in a way, both exiles, our real homes far from this small, rather impersonal island in the Channel.

He had read widely, and sympathized with my ambitions to be a writer. He had tried it once himself, and failed.

'I didn't have the perseverance, lad,' he said. 'I wasn't inventive enough, either. It isn't enough to be able to write well—you have to know how to tell a good story . . . Those who could do both, like Conrad and Stevenson, those are the ones we still read today. The critics keep telling us that Henry James was a master stylist, and so he was, but who reads Henry James?'

Mr Bromley rather admired my naive but determined attempt to write a book.

On a Sunday afternoon I was standing in front of a shop, gazing wistfully at a baby portable typewriter on display. It was just what I wanted. My book was nearly finished but I knew I'd have to get it typed before submitting it to a publisher.

'Buying a typewriter, lad?' Mr Bromley had stopped beside me.

'I wish I could,' I said. 'But it's £19 and I've only got £6 saved up. I'll have to hire some old machine.'

'But a good-looking typescript can make a world of difference, lad. Editors are jaded people. If they find a dirty manuscript on the desk, they feel like chucking it in the wastepaper basket—even if it is a masterpiece!'

'There's an old typewriter belonging to my aunt,' I said, 'but it should be in a museum. The letter 'b' is missing. She must have used that one a lot—or perhaps it was my uncle. Anyway, when I type my stories on it, I have to go through them again and ink in all the missing b's.'

'That won't do, lad. I tell you what, though. Give me your £6 and I'll add £13 to it, and we'll buy the machine. Then you can pay me back out of your wages—a pound every week. How would that suit you?'

I accepted his offer and walked down the street in

a state of euphoria, the gleaming new typewriter in my hand. I sat up late that night, hammering out the first chapter of my book.

It was midsummer then, and by the end of the year I had paid £6 back to Mr Bromley. It was then that I received a letter from a publisher (the third to whom I had submitted the book) saying that they had liked my story, but had some suggestions to make, and could I call on them in London?

I took a few days' leave and crossed the Channel to England.

London swept me me off my feet. The theatres and bookshops exerted their magic on me. And the publishers said they would take my book if only I'd try writing it again.

At eighteen, I was prepared to rewrite a book a dozen times, so I took a room in Hampstead, and grabbed the first job that came my way. I would have to keep working until I established myself as a writer. I did not know, then, how long this would take, but life was only just beginning, and I fell in love with someone, and someone fell in love with me, and both loves were unrequited; but all the same I was very happy.

For some time I was unable to send any money to Mr Bromley. My wage was small, and London was expensive. I meant to write to him, explaining the situation, but kept putting it off, telling myself that I would write as soon as I had some money to send him.

Several months passed, I wrote the book a third time, and this time it was accepted and I received a modest advance. I opened an account with Lloyd's, and the first cheque I made out was in the name of Mr Bromley.

But it was never to be cashed. It came back in the post with my letter, and along with it was letter from my former employer saying that Mr Bromley had gone away and left no address. It seemed to me that he had given up his quest for better health, and had gone home to his own part of the country.

And so my debt was never paid.

The typewriter is still with me. I have used it for over ten years, and it is now old and battered. But I will not give it away. It's like a guilty conscience, always beside me, always reminding me to pay my debts in time.

read—and get well

Most people, when they fall ill, manage to get well (or worse) with the help of drugs, modern or traditional. There are a few, like the amazing Morarji Desai, who thrive on nature's bounty—nuts and fruits and health-giving herbs, apart from the 'water of life' which really ought to be taken more seriously. And some practise Yoga for health and longevity, while others go to faith healers and miraclemen. Even hypnosis and magnetism are given a try. And why not? We are all made differently, and what is a curse to you may be a cure for me!

One of the most effective forms of healing has, I think, been largely neglected both by doctors and patients, that's healing by reading.

Have you tried it? If you are in the dumps or in bed with a bug, or recovering from a serious illness, or waiting for a fracture to heal, get hold of a book or books by your favourite author, and read as much as you can. You will start feeling better far sooner than if you simply lie on your back and feel sorry for yourself. A book cannot prevent illness or injury (although a book in the pocket has been known to deflect a bullet!) but it can certainly help in the process of recovery.

Now I learn that psychiatrists are placing great importance on the choice of reading matter for patient who are mentally ill. While they all agree that reading is beneficial, they also point out that it is possible to be given the wrong sort of book—just as you can, unintentionally, be given the wrong sort of medicine!

For instance, a mental patient suffering from homicidal tendencies should not be given *Crime and Punishment* or a biography of *The Boston Strangler*. The urge to get up and strangle your doctor might well manifest itself. More soothing authors, like Jane Austen or Henry James, should be prescribed. If they put the patient to sleep, all the better.

Religious books are of course a comfort to most people, and there's nothing like a passage from the Gita or one of David's Psalms to dispel gloom and depression. When things aren't going too well for me, I consult the *I Ching*, and usually get the right sort of wisdom and advice. Not so long ago, when I was suffering all the pangs of a rejected lover, I consulted the *Book of Change* and under the appropriate hexagram found the following lines:

'If you lose your horse, do not run after it,
It will come back of its own accord.'

I stopped chasing, and the object of my affections (please don't think it was a horse!) did indeed return.

I remember when, as a boy, I went abroad, I suffered so much from homesickness for India that I made myself ill and ended up in a London hospital with jaundice and an eye disease. It took me a month to be up and about again, but it would have taken much longer if a kind friend hadn't brought me a bunch of books which he thought might cheer me up. One of these was by a now neglected writer, Sudhin Ghose, called *And Gazelles Leaping*. It was a delightful autobiographical story about a sensitive boy growing up in rural Bengal. Reading it, I was determined to get well and return to India.

Another book that helped me was Jerome K. Jerome's *Three Men in a Boat*. I think Jawaharlal Nehru used to read it when he was in jail. Well, I was only in hospital, but it certainly made me feel perfectly able to get up and make my way down to the little pub across the road.

Is it just a coincidence that in the so-called developed countries the incidence of mental illness has risen alongside the decline in reading habits and the increase in TV-watching? In the not-too-distant future, when everyone is glued to a TV set, wearing TV-slippers and eating a TV-supper with a TV-husband or wife, perhaps a book will be just another doctor's prescription for getting back your sanity.

At least it's safe. I have yet to hear of anyone dying from an overdose of reading.

the evil eye

In northern India, it is called *nazar*—a glance of malice or envy—and it is held accountable for a wide variety of ailments and disasters.

Recently the milkman's cow went dry. His excuse: his neighbour, who also kept a cow, had been jealous and cast an evil eye which was enough to end the competition! And then there is the man who tells me that his ailing child is growing thinner day by day because a childless person has cast the evil eye upon him.

I do not scoff at these beliefs. Ill will and evil intent

cannot be shrugged off lightly. Hate has an aura which quickly permeates the surroundings.

When members of my own household underwent a series of disasters, I was puzzled at the way in which they followed rapidly one after another. Only later did I learn that someone had actually been wishing ill upon us. We were the victims of *nazar*— a baleful glance from the evil eye of someone who passed us on the road every day.

In India, as in most countries, the popular explanation for the fairly widespread belief in the evil eye is that it is based on envy or covetousness. It is logical enough to suppose that a man with only one eye is likely to envy a man who has two; the weak and puny envy the good health and good looks of others; the childless woman covets the children of more fortunate women.

One is not surprised to learn that in the ancient Hindu 'Laws of Manu', a one-eyed man is classed with those who are to be treated with caution, possibly because his glance is more concentrated than that of a man with sight in both eyes.

The old prejudice against the one-eyed resulted in Maha Singh, one of the Jaisalmer princes, being disqualified from succeeding to the throne. And when Jaswant Rao Holkar, another powerful Indian prince lost one of his eyes, he remarked: 'I was thought bad enough before—now I shall be looked upon as a guru among rogues!'

The prejudice extends even today to persons with a squint or cast in the eye. Years ago, I knew of an office clerk who suffered from a squint—and the accounts of his fellow clerks always went wrong. They made so many mistakes in their work that they compelled him to cover the offending eye with a cloth during office hours.

The belief that certain persons possess the power of discharging a glance so malefic that it strikes like a dart at the person against whom it is directed, is prevalent in many parts of the world. Many believe that those born on a Saturday, under the unhappy influence of Saturn, have the power to cast an evil eye.

This worldwide belief comes down from remote antiquity. The English word 'fascination' is from the Latin *fascinatio*, which is transliterated from the classical Greek word meaning 'the mysterious bewitching power of the evil eye'. The ancient Egyptians knew and feared the evil eye, carried mascots and muttered protective charms as do the Bedouins and Moors even today.

Montague Summers, the great English student of

the occult (whose book *The Vampire* is a classic work), once described how, on a visit to Italy, he was walking with an Italian friend down the Via Roma, the main street of Naples, when he noticed people suddenly begin to scatter in every direction. His friend took him firmly by the arm and guided him into the nearest shop.

'What on earth is up?' asked Summers.

'*Zitto, zitto*,' whispered his friend, putting a finger to his lips.

A tall, well-dressed man, quite a respectable-looking figure, was walking along the empty pavement past the shop window. Summers heard the word '*Jettatore*' and saw the protective gesture, the pointing horns, made with the hands of those who got out of the mysterious man in the street.

In Italy a '*Jettatore*' is a man (or woman) with the evil eye; one whose mere presence, whose very shadow, is ill-omened and unlucky enough, but whose baleful glance brings sorrow, sickness and death. Such a person may often be quite unaware of the effect he has on others.

In parts of rural England, sickly or deformed children are still spoken of as *wisht*—that is, 'ill-wished' or 'overlooked', injured by someone who has cast his or her malevolent gaze upon the sufferer.

An old woman in Somerset once quoted to me from the Bible (proverbs, XXIII. 6): 'Eat not the bread of him that hath an evil eye ... The morsel which thou hast eaten shalt thou vomit up.'

And she added: 'There's more than one of my neighbours I wouldn't sit down to eat a meal with!'

In Europe you ward off the evil eye by 'making horns'—tucking in the thumb and extending the first and little fingers. In India, one method of avoiding the evil eye is to make on the person likely to be effected a mark which acts as a disguise or distraction. Many people apply *kajal* (lampblack) to their children's eyes, a device which also serves the practical purpose of protecting them from sunglare! Or a spot is marked in the middle of the forehead, like a third eye—rather like the false 'eyes' on the wings of butterflies, which are meant to distract predatory birds.

Even domestic animals, like cattle and horses are protected by having brightly coloured beads round their necks or by marking part of the harness with a single of double triangle. A horse is similarly safeguarded by leaving in the courtyard an earthen pot smeared with streaks of black and white.

Strings and knots, tattooing, precious stones, iron rings made of silver and gold, incense, various grasses or herbs, saliva, blood ... all have magical or protective properties.

Garlic has been used as a protective in both the East and West. Count Dracula's hypnotic eye was powerless in the presence of a liberal amount of garlic! And in parts of central India, before a young man's marriage, an exorcist crushes pieces of garlic near his eyes or squeezes the juice into his nostrils to expel any evil spirit that might be lurking within.

In some parts of northern India, children who have been the victims of the evil eye are said to be cured by waving garlic and pepper-pods round their heads on a Tuesday; these are then thrown into the fire.

Lest all this be dismissed as mere superstition, it would be well to recall that the power of positive and negative thinking has time and again been proved by scientists. In one study, identical barley seeds were planted in pots containing the same soil. All were similarly watered and exposed to sunlight for the same amount of time. But one set received positive thoughts directed at it; the other set received negative thoughts; and the third was left alone.

After fourteen days it was found that the 'blessed' seeds grew slightly better than the ones which received no thoughts at all. The most remarkable thing, however, was that the seeds which were 'cursed' grew only half the size of the others and 62 per cent did not even germinate.

Before scoffing at the power of the evil eye, ponder upon the feats of hypnotism. A powerful mind, using the intensifying apparatus of the eye, is able to influence a mind open to suggestion.

Surely the best way to deal with a baleful glance or negative thought is to reverse the roles, and draw upon one's own latent powers of suggestion, challenge the evil eye, stare it down, set it at naught. Meet it with a steadfast eye!

And should you find a staring match too much of a strain, here's a trick my magic-making grandmother taught me: *Don't* stare the other person in the eye. Fix your gaze on a point *between* the eyes, on the bridge of the nose, and keep it there. Your opponent will look away.

these i have loved

Seashells ... they are among my earliest memories. I was five years old, walking barefoot along the golden sand of a Kathiawar beach, collecting shells and cowries and taking them home to fill up an old trunk. Some of these shells remained with me through the years, and I still have one; whenever I put it to my ear I can listen to the distant music of the Arabian Sea.

A jackfruit tree. It stood outside my grandfather's house in Dehradun, in northern India; it was easy to climb, and generous with the shade it provided; and in its trunk was large hole where I kept my marble, sweets, prohibited books, and other treasures.

I have always like the smell of certain leaves, even more than the scent of flowers. Crushed geranium leaves, mint, myrtle, the leaves of marigolds, lime, and neem trees after rain. I am always looking for these leaves, so that I might smell them.

Of course there were other smells which, as a boy, I especially liked—the smells of *pillaus* and *kofta* curries, roast chicken and fried fish. But these are smells loved by most gourmets (and most boys), and are not as personal as the smells of leaves and grass.

As a schoolboy I travelled to Simla in the little train that crawls round and through the mountains. In March the flowers on the rhododendron trees would provide splashes of red against the dark green of the hills. Sometimes there would be snow on the ground to add to the contrast.

What else do I love and remember of the Himalayas? Smells, again ... The smell of fallen pine needles, cow-dung smoke, spring rain, bruised grass. The pure water of mountain streams, the depth and blueness of the sky—enchanted things that are common to mountains almost everywhere.

I liked trains and railway stations. I liked eating at railway stations, a liking I carried with me to England.

At Indian railway stations I ate hot gram, peanuts, and oranges. At British railway-stations I frequented the buffet-restaurants, where I had buns or muffins, and mugs of hot but rather tasteless tea.

In the hills, I have loved forests. In the plains, the single trees. A lone tree on a wide flat plain—even if it is a thin, crooked, nondescript tree—gains nobility from its very isolation, from the precarious nature of its existence.

Of course I have had my favourites among trees. The banyan, with its great branches spreading to form roots and intricate passageways. The peepul, with its beautiful heart-shaped leaf catching the breeze and fluttering even on the stillest of days. It is always cool under the peepul. The jacaranda and the gulmohur, bursting into blossom with the coming of summer. The cherries, peaches and apricots flowering in the hills, the handsome chestnuts and whispering deodars.

And which flower is most redolent of India, of the heat and light and colour of India? Not the lotus or the water lily, but the simple marigold, fresh, golden, dew-drenched, kissed by the morning sun.

The smell of the sea. I lived with it for a year, in the Channel Islands. I liked the sea-mist, and I liked the fierce gales that swept across the islands in the winter.

Later, there were the fogs of London; I did not like them, but they made me think of Dickens, and I walked to Wapping and the East India Dock Road, and watched the barges on the Thames. I had my favourite pub, and my favourite fish and chip shop.

There are always children flying kites from Primrose Hill, or sailing boats in the ponds on Hampstead Heath. And in a hothouse at Kew, moist and smelling of the tropics, I remembered the East and the simple things I had known; a field of wheat, a stack of sugar cane, a cow at rest, and a boy sleeping in the shade of a long red-fingered poinsettia ...

These are some of the things I have loved.

when time stands still

If there be a heaven on earth, it is this, it is this. The words are inscribed on the wall of the *Diwan-i-Khas*, or the Hall of Private Audience, in the royal gardens of the Red Fort at Delhi, built by Shah Jahan in the seventeenth century. It is a beautiful pavillion, the walls inlaid with jade and other semi-precious stones, and from the latticed windows one sees the waters of the Jamuna winding placidly across the plain.

In Shah Jahan's time, the river ran much closer to the fort and I like to think that the Emperor, when he found time to be alone, strolled along the ramparts of his palace while it was being constructed; and that one evening, while he gazed at the river, something happened to make him feel at peace with the world and he was so moved by his surroundings that he decided to build his private pavillion at that spot, inscribing on its walls the words, or rather the poetry, that came to him that moment of truth: 'If there be a heaven on earth, it is this, it is this . . .'

Such moments come to each of us, moments when we feel deeply moved or inspired, moments when time seems to stand still, or when we become acutely aware of the benediction of sun and wind and trees. These moments of great wonder and delight are, for me, rare. They come as small miracles, like the fragrance of the first summer rain on the parched earth, or the song of the whistling thrush emerging like a sweet secret from a dark forest—moments when heaven is here, compensating for the irritations and disasters that we build around ourselves each day.

When I was seventeen, I wanted desperately to be a writer but my early efforts did not meet much success and my relatives threw cold water on my aspirations. At that time I was living and working in Jersey, in the Channel Islands. Late one evening, when I was feeling particularly depressed, I went out for a walk along the seafront. The tide was in, the sea was rough, and the wind which was almost a gale came pouring in from the darkness like a mad genie just released from his bottle. Great waves crashed against the sea-wall and the wind whipped the salt spray into my face, I was alone in a wild wasteland of wind and water. And then something touched me, something from the elements took hold of my heart, and all the stuffing went out of my head, and I felt as free and as virile as the wind. I spoke to the genie in the swirling darkness and said; 'I will be writer, I am going to write, and no one can stop me.'

A week later, with a capital of five pounds and ten shillings (then equal to about a hundred rupees), I left my astonished relatives and went to live in London, where the writing began again. It is still going on, and it is still a struggle. But whenever I feel like giving up, I try to recapture that moment when heaven and earth and I were all one, and when I remember, the writing begins again.

Heaven seems to turn up when we least expect it. A few years ago, I gave up a good job in Delhi and came to live in a hill station, partly because I love mountains and forests, and partly because I wanted to devote more time to writing. I live at the edge of a forest of oak and maple. I am happy among trees but the full magic of a tree was only brought home to me just over a year ago when I was in the plains.

I was walking through a stretch of wasteland, a

desert that seemed to stretch endlessly across a wide, flat plain. Just as I was beginning to find the heat and the glare a little discouraging, I saw a tree, just one small, crooked tree shimmering in the distance. And seeing it there all by itself, but growing stubbornly where other trees would not grow, I was filled with love and admiration for it. When I reached the tree, I found that it had given shelter to other small plants from the sun. A pair of parrots emerged from a hole in the tree trunk and flew across the plain, flashes of red and green and gold. Finding that tree there, struggling on its own but giving life to other things, was like finding a bit of heaven where I least expected it.

I decided that people, even in large numbers, could be good to live with and that Thoreau must have missed a lot when he turned his back on people and went to live alone in the woods.

Almost always, it's the unexpected that delights us, that takes us by the throat and gives us a good shaking, leaving us gaping in wonder. It may only be a shaft of sunlight slanting through the pillars of a banyan tree or dewdrops caught in a spider's web or, in the stillness of the mountains, the sudden chatter of a mountain stream as you round the bend of a hill. Or an emperor's first glimpse of a winding river and the world beyond.

from a window

The sitting-room window opened out on to the forest, but my bedroom window faced the hillside and offered a more limited though equally interesting view.

A wild cherry tree had grown out of the *pushta*, or retaining wall, and in a strong wind its branches would beat against the window as though it wanted to get in. Unlike most fruit trees, it blossomed in November—pale pink blossoms that covered the tree for about a fortnight. Later, when the fruit appeared, small birds would arrive to feast on the sour wild cherries. Bulbuls, warblers, brightly coloured finches. The tree inspired me to write a story in which little Rakesh, Prem's three-year-old son, featured. Prem's family was to grow steadily over the years, and today Rakesh is a married man with three children of his own. There is also Mukesh and his family; and their sister Dolly ... All my family over the years, and thirty-five years on I'm the twelfth man, occasionally carrying out the drinks and doing the fielding.

But to return to the window. From my bed I could see the tree and beyond it, the little path that came down the steep hillside up to my front door. I couldn't see the entire pathway, but far enough to know who was approaching—tradesman, or postman, or neighbour, or casual visitor.

If I was not in the mood for a casual visitor, there would be time to warn Prem and he would meet the caller and say I was out for the day. People who did not know me always seemed to call in the afternoon, in the middle of my siesta. It still happens. I don't mind being disturbed while I'm eating or working or bathing, but siesta time is sacred and I'm very grumpy then—like a bear disturbed during his long winter sleep.

And yet, I'm happy to be up at four or five in the morning to watch the coming of the dawn.

In some earlier life (if there was one) I might well have been a worshipper of Ushas, the goddess of the dawn. In the Rig Veda, that first pale flush of light is compared to a mother awakening her children; to a lovely maiden awakening a sleeping world. She is described as the giver of light, ever youthful, ever receiving.

If, today, we all become worshippers of Usha, everyone would rise at dawn, start the day's work at six or seven, and come home to rest at noon. Then we would all enjoy afternoon siestas and no one would disturb me.

love your art

'Love the art, poor as it may be, which thou hast learned, and be content with it; and pass through the rest of life like one who has entrusted to the gods with his whole soul and all that he has, making thyself neither the tyrant nor the slave of any man.'

Marcus Aurelius (121–180 A.D.) the last of the great Antonian Emperors, speaks to us across the centuries through his *Meditations*, nuggets of wisdom jotted down during a crowded and adventurous life.

Being unable to find much comfort or wisdom in the utterances of present-day teachers, preachers, or godmen (be they of the Eastern or Western variety), I frequently turn for advice and reassurance to the early Greek and Roman philosophers—Epicurus (341–270 BC) Epictetus (a little later), Marcus Aurelius, Seneca and others—those Stoics and Epicureans whose precepts are as relevant today as they were during the finest flowering of the Greek and Roman civilizations.

'Love your art, poor as it may be . . .' I have never regretted following this precept; for no matter how skillful one is with words, it is only drudgery to have to use them in the more mundane spheres of journalism. I have tried to use words creatively and lovingly. The gift for putting together words and sentences to make stories or poems or essays has carried me through life with a certain serenity and inner harmony which could not have come from any unloved vocation.

Within my own 'art' I think I have known my limitations and worked within them, thus sparing myself the bitter disappointment that comes to those whose ambitions stretch far beyond their talents. Do what you know best, and do it well. Act impeccably. Eveything will then fall into place.

I was looking for a living example to try and illustrate this precept, and came across it in the persons of Mahboob Khan and Ramji Mal, stone-masons who were engaged in restoring Shah Jahan's Hall of Mirrors in the Agra Fort. They had been at work for ten years, slowly but deftly bringing their epic task to completion.

The restoration work is so intricate that these two skilled craftsmen could restore only about six inches in a day. In recreating the original stucco-work on walls and ceiling, everything has to be done impeccably; millions of pieces of tiny mirrors and coloured glass have to find their exact place in order to reflect just the right amount of light and, at the same time, conform to a certain pattern.

It is a small art, theirs, but it requires infinite patience, skill and dedication. No fame for them, no great material reward. Their greatest reward comes from the very act of taking pains in the pursuit of perfection.

Surely they must be happy, or at least contented men. In truth, I have yet to meet a neurotic carpenter or stonemason or clay-worker or bangle maker or master craftsman of any kind. Those who work with wood or stone or glass—those who fashion beautiful things with their hands—are usually well-balanced people. Working with the hands is in itself a therapy. Those of us who work with our minds—composers or artists or writers—must try to emulate these craftsmen's methods, paying attention to every detail and working with loving care.

The trouble is that creative people are cerebral creatures with fluctuations of mood that make life exhilarating one moment and depressing the next. And this is often reflected in their work unless they have become machines, turning out books or paintings like *samosas*.

Yet there are times when I do love my art. And because I have loved it, I think I have been able to pass through life without being any man's slave or tyrant.

bird life in the city

Having divided the last ten years of my life between Delhi and Mussoorie, I have come to the heretical conclusion that there is more bird life in the cities than there is in the hills and forests around our hill stations.

For birds to survive, they must learn to live with and off humans; and those birds, like crows, sparrow and mynas, who do this to perfection, continue to thrive as our cities grow; whereas the purely wild birds, those who depend upon the forests for life, are rapidly disappearing, simply because the forests are disappearing.

Recently, I saw more birds in one week in a New Delhi colony than I had seen during a month in the hills. Here, one must be patient and alert if one is to spot just a few of the birds so beautifully described in Salim Ali's *Indian Hill Birds*. The babblers and thrushes are still around, but the flycatchers and warblers are seldom seen or heard.

In Delhi, if you have just a bit of garden and perhaps a guava tree, you will be visited by innumerable bulbuls, tailorbirds, mynas, hoopoes, parrots and tree pies. Or, if you own an old house, you will have to share it with pigeons and sparrows, perhaps swallows or swifts. And if you have neither garden nor rooftop, you will still be visited by the crows.

Where the man goes, the crow follows. He has learnt to perfection the art of living off humans. He will, I am sure, be the first bird on the moon, scavenging among the paper bags and cartons left behind by untidy astronauts.

Crows favour the densest areas of human

population, and there must be at least one for every human. Many crows seem to have been humans in their previous lives; they possess all the cunning and sense of self-preservation of man. At the same time, there are many humans who have obviously been crows; we haven't lost their thieving instincts.

Watch a crow sidling along the garden wall with a shabby genteel air, cocking a speculative eye at the kitchen door and any attendant humans. He reminds one of a newspaper reporter, hovering in the background until his chance comes—and then pouncing! I have even known a crow to make off with an egg from the breakfast table. No other bird, except perhaps the sparrow, has been so successful in exploiting human beings.

The myna, although he too is quite at home in the city, is more of a gentleman. He prefers fruit on the tree to scraps from the kitchen, and visits the garden as much out of a sense of sociability as in expectation of hand-outs. He is quite handsome, too, with his bright orange bill and the mask around his eyes. He is equally at home on a railway platform as on the ear of a grazing buffalo, and, being omnivorous, has no trouble in coexisting with man.

The sparrow, on the other hand, is not a gentleman. Uninvited, he enters your home, followed by his friends, relatives and political hangers-on, and proceeds to quarrel, make love and leave his droppings on the sofa-cushions, with a complete disregard for the presence of humans. The party will then proceed into the garden and destroy all the flower-buds. No birds have succeeded so well in making fools of humans.

Although the bluejay, or roller, is quite capable of making his living in the forest, he seems to show a preference for the haunts of men, and would rather perch on a telegraph wire than in a tree. Probably he finds the wire a better launching pad for his sudden rocket-flights and aerial acrobatics.

In repose he is rather shabby; but in flight, when his outspread wings reveal his brilliant blues, he takes one's breath away. As his food consists of beetles and other insect pests, he can be considered man's friend and ally.

Parrots make little or no distinction between town and country life. They are the freelances of the bird world—sturdy, independent and noisy. With flashes of blue and green, they swoop across the road, settle for a while in a mango tree, and then, with shrill delighted cries, move on to some other field or orchard.

They will sample all the fruit they can, without

finishing any. They are destructive birds but, because of their bright plumage, graceful flight and charming ways, they are popular favourites and can get away with anything. No one who has enjoyed watching a flock of parrots in swift and carefree flight could want to cage one of these virile birds. Yet so many people do cage them.

After the peacock, perhaps the most popular bird in rural India is the sarus crane—a familiar sight around the *jheels* and river banks of northern India and Gujarat. The sarus pairs for life and is seldom seen without his mate. When one bird dies, the other often pines away and seemingly dies of grief. It is this near-human quality of devotion that has earned the birds their popularity with the villagers of the plains.

As a result, they are well protected.

In the long run, it is the 'common man', and not the scientist or conservationist, who can best give protection to the birds and animals living around him. Religious sentiment has helped preserve the peacock and a few other birds. It is a pity that so many other equally beautiful birds do not enjoy the same protection.

But the wily crow, the cheeky sparrow, and the sensible myna will always be with us. Quite possibly they will survive the human species.

And it is the same with other animals. While the cringing jackal has learnt the art of survival, his master, the magnificent tiger, is on his way to extinction.

letter to my father

My Dear Dad,

Last week I decided to walk from the Dilaram Bazaar to Rajpur, a walk I hadn't undertaken for many years. It's only about five miles, a long straight tree-lined road, houses most of the way, but here and there are open spaces where there are fields and patches of sal forest. The road hasn't changed much, but there is far more traffic than there used to be, which makes it noisy and dusty, detracting from the sylvan surroundings. All the same I enjoyed the walk—enjoyed the cool breeze that came down from the hills—the rich variety of trees, the splashes of colour where bougainvillea trailed over porches and verandahs—enjoyed the passing cyclists and bullock carts, for they were reminders of the old days when cars, trucks and buses were the exception rather than the rule.

A little way above the Dilaram Bazaar, just where the canal goes under the road, stands the old house we used to know as Melville Hall, where three generations of Melvilles had lived. It is now a government office and looks dirty and neglected. Beside it still stands the little cottage, or guest house, where you stayed for a few weeks while the separation from my mother was being made legal. Then I went to live with you in Delhi.

At the time you were a guest of the Melvilles, I was in boarding-school, so I did not share the cottage with you, although I was to share a number of rooms, tents and RAF hutments with you during the next two or three years. But of course I knew the Melvilles—I would visit them during school holidays in the years after you died, and they always spoke affectionately of you. One of the sisters was particularly kind to me; I think it was she who gave you the use of the cottage. This was Mrs Chill—she'd lost her husband to cholera during their honeymoon, and never married again. But I always found her cheerful and good-natured, loading me with presents on birthdays and at Christmas. The kindest people are often those who have come through testing personal tragedies.

A young man on a bicycle stops beside me and asks if I remember him.

'Not with that terrible moustache,' I confess.

'Romi, from Sisters Bazaar.'

Yes, of course. And I do remember him, although it must be about ten years since we last met; he was just a schoolboy then. Now, he tells me, he's a teacher. Not very well paid, as he works in a small private school. But better than being unemployed, he says. I have to agree.

'You're a good teacher, I'm sure, Romi. And it's still a noble profession.'

He looks pleased as he cycles away.

When I see boys on bicycles I am always taken back to my boyhood days in Dehra. The roads in those uncrowded days were ideal for cyclists. Somi on his bicycle, riding down this very road in the light spring rain, provided me with the opening scene for my very first novel, *The Room on the Roof*, written a couple of years after I'd said goodbye to Somi and Dehra and even, for a time, India.

That's how I remember him best—on his bicycle, wearing shorts, turban slightly askew, always a song on his lips. He was just fifteen. I was a couple of years older, but I wasn't much of a bicycle rider, always falling off the machine when I was supposed to dismount gracefully. On one occasion I went sailing into a buffalo-cart and fractured my forearm. Last year when Dr Murti, a senior citizen of the Doon, met me at a local function, he recalled how he had set my arm forty years ago. He was so nice to me that I forbore from telling him that my arm was still crooked.

Strictly an earth man, I have never really felt at ease with my feet off the ground. That's why I've been a walking person for most of my life. In planes, on ships, even in lifts, panic sets in.

As it did on that occasion when I was four or five, and you, Dad, decided to give me a treat by taking me on an Arab dhow across the Gulf of Kutch. Five minutes on that swinging, swaying sailing ship, was enough for me; I became so hysterical that I had to be taken off and rowed back to port. Not that the rowing boat was much better.

And then my mother thought I should go up with her in one those four-winged aeroplanes, a Tiger Moth I think—there's a photograph of it somewhere among my mementos—one of those contraptions that fell out of the sky without much assistance during the first World War. I think you could make them at home. Anyway, in this too I kicked and screamed with such abandon that the poor pilot had to be content with taxiing around the airfield and dropping me off at the first opportunity. That same plane with the same pilot, crashed a couple of months later, only reinforcing my fears about machines that could not stay anchored to the ground.

To return to Somi, he was one of those friends I never saw again as an adult, so he remains transfixed in my memory as eternal youth, dream-bright, forever loving ... Meeting boyhood friends again after long intervals can often be disappointing, even disconcerting. Mere survival leaves its mark. Success is even more disfiguring. Those who climb to the top of a profession, or who seek the pinnacles of power, usually have to pay a heavy price for it, both physically and spiritually. It sounds like a cliche but it's true that money can't buy good health or a serene state of mind—especially the latter. You can fly to the ends of the earth in search of the best climate or the best medical treatment, and the chances are that you will have to keep flying! Poverty is not ennobling—far from it—but it does at least teach you to make the most out of very little.

I have often dreamt of Somi, and it is always the same dream, year after year, for over forty years. We meet in a fairground, set up on Dehra's old parade-ground which has seen better days. In the dream I am a man but he is still a boy. We wander through the fairground, enjoying all that it has to offer, and when the dream ends we are still in that fairground which probably represents heaven.

Heaven. Is that the real heaven—the perfect place with the perfect companion? And if you and I meet again, Dad, will you look the same, and will I be a small boy or an old man?

In my dreams of you I meet you on a busy street, after many lost years, and you receive me with the same old warmth, but where were you all those missing years? A traveller in another dimension, perhaps, returning occasionally just to see if I am all right.

Ruskin Bond

flattery, thy name is success

When I was a boy in Dehra, there was a mango-grove just opposite the bungalow. It belonged to someone called Seth Govind Ram (may his soul rest in peace), and, during the mango season, it was fiercely guarded by a giant of a man called Phambiri. All my efforts to get into the grove were repulsed, and on one occasion I received a mild lathi-blow on my back.

'I just wanted to climb the tree,' I pleaded.

'Come back when the mango season is over,' said

Phambiri with a smile which reminded me of a filmi villain.

I discovered he was an ex-wrestler, that he had been a champion in his youth, and had even thrown the great King Kong out of the ring. (I did not know at the time that King Kong, in his bad years, was constantly being thrown out of the ring). So, whenever I passed the grove and saw Phambiri, I would remark on his great strength, his superb condition, his muscles like cricket balls, and his bull-like neck and shoulders. Gradually he warmed to me, and began to tell me of his exploits. I acclaimed them. Then he showed me feats of strength, like picking up rocks and hurling them across the road, I applauded. Before long, he had invited me into the mango-grove, and by the end of the week I could have all the mangoes I wanted.

Flattery will get you anywhere. One of the first lessons learnt by schoolchildren is that the majority of teachers are susceptible to the most blatant forms of flattery. Hard work helps a little, but the child at the top of the class is often held in esteem by a teacher for being 'so polite, so sweet, such a little gentleman', etc. This paragon of virtue wears an adoring smile, and always waits till the teacher is out of hearing before slandering her. 'They do but flatter with their lips, and disemble in their double heart.'

The Psalmist was speaking of political hangers-on, but he could have been talking of schoolchildren. Their power games are played out on similar lines.

But why pick on children? Great lovers throughout the ages have flattered their way into the hearts of their beloveds. Napoleon may have been overdoing it a bit when he breathed heavily down Marie Waleska's neck and blurted out: 'I have seen only you. I have admired only you. I desire only you.' All the same, she succumbed.

Men are no less susceptible ... Lady Hamilton wrote to Lord Nelson: 'When you are here, it will be paradise.' Nelson did his best to be there.

There is of course that cynical old play of telling a woman she looks ten years younger than her actual age. This doesn't always work. I once told a woman (who looked fifty) that she looked an attractive forty, and she hit me over the ear with her handbag. It turned out that she was thirty.

Be careful when you flatter. The results can sometimes be unexpected.

a place of peace and power

On the first clear day of October, I visited the pine-knoll, my place of peace and power.

It was months since I had last been there. Trips to the plains, a crisis in my affairs, involvements with other people and their troubles, and an entire monsoon had come between me and the grassy, pine-topped slope facing the eternal snows of the Himalayas. Now I tramped through autumn foliage— tall ferns, wild balsam, bushes festooned with flowering convolvulus—crossed the stream by way of the little bridge of stones, and climbed the steep hill to the pine slope.

When the trees saw me, they made as if to turn in my direction. A puff to wind came across the valley from the distant snows. A long-tailed blue magpie took alarm and flew noisily out of an oak tree. The cicadas were suddenly silent. But the trees remembered me. They bowed gently in the breeze and beckoned me nearer, welcoming me home. Three pines, a straggling oak, and a wild cherry. I went among them, acknowledged their welcome with a touch of my hand against their trunks—the cherry's smooth and polished; the pine's patterned and whorled; the oak's rough, gnarled, full of experience. He had been there the longest, and the wind had bent his upper branches and twisted a few, so that he looked shaggy and undistinguished. But, like the philosopher who is careless about his dress and appearance, the oak has secrets, a hidden wisdom. He has learnt the art of survival.

While the oak and the pines are older than me and have been here many years, the cherry tree is exactly ten years old. I know, because I planted it.

One day I had this cherry seed in my hand, and on an impulse I thrust it into the soft earth and then went away and forgot all about it. A few months later I found a tiny cherry tree in the long grass. I did not expect it to survive. But the following year it was two feet tall. And then some goats ate the young leaves, and a grasscutter's scythe injured the stem, and I was sure the tree would wither away. But it renewed itself, sprang up even faster; and within three years it was a healthy growing tree, about five feet tall.

I left the hills for a few years—forced by circumstances to make a living in the plains—but this time I did not forget the cherry tree. I thought about it quite often, sending it telepathic messages of love and encouragement. And when, last year, I returned in the autumn, my heart did a somersault when I found my tree sprinkled with pale pink blossom. (The Himalayan cherry flowers in November). Later, when the fruit was ripe, the tree was visited by finches, tits, bulbuls, and other small birds, all coming to feast on the sour red cherries.

Last summer I spent a night on the pine-knoll, sleeping on the grass beneath the cherry tree. I lay awake for hours, listening to the chatter of the stream and the occasional tonk-tonk of a nightjar; and watching, through the branches overhead, the stars turning in the sky and earth, and the power of a small cherry seed . . .

And so, when the rains are over, this is where I come, that I might feel the peace and power of this magic place. It's a big world, and momentous events are taking place all the time. But this is where I have seen it happen.

bibliophiles and book worms

We have in our part of the world both book-lovers and book-borrowers (and even a few buyers), but very few collectors—the latter being a set of enthusiasts found in small but effective numbers in Europe and the United States.

The collecting of books—modern or early first editions, rare books on travel, natural history, medicine, early illuminated manuscripts, and medieval books with embossed bindings—has been developed to the same degree of specialization as stamp-collecting, with the difference that there is more intrinsic merit in a book than in a postage stamp. For some, collecting books is a pastime; but for the bibliophile it is a passon, almost a crusade, and the collector will go to a lot of trouble and expense in order to obtain a rare item.

The number of collectors who will spend a small fortune on rare, out-of-print books has increased over the years, especially in America, where many libraries of great value have found a home. The price of an individual item may be anything from two rupees to several lakhs of rupees, depending on rarity, literary and aesthetic value, its antecedents and condition. At a sale in July this year, Herrick's *Commonplace Book* fetched almost Rs 5 lakhs.

Rarity is in itself no criterion. Book-collecting has been defined by John Carter as 'the bringing together of books which in their contents, their form or the history of the individual copy possess some elements of personal interest . . . and are rare in the sense of being difficult to procure'. But perhaps the best definition of a rare book is 'a book I want and can't find'.

There would be more bibliophiles in India if paper did not have so many natural enemies. The climate itself has a destructive effect. The damp, the dust, the large number of insects and rodents who have a special fondness for paper (preferring old paper to new) take a toll of books already delicate with age. I have sometimes come across a rare item, only to have my enthusiasm dampened by the discovery that half the book has been eaten away by some obnoxious book worm or weevil.

However, valuable finds can and have been made in India. Several years ago a first edition of *Alice in Wonderland* was discovered in a second-hand Bangalore bookstore. It was purchased for a rupee and later sold at a London auction for £880!

This, however, was an exceptional find. But should anyone be lucky enough to find an early Kipling in good condition—especially one of Wheeler's Indian Railway Library editions of the stories published in the 1890's *Wee Willie Winkie, The Phantom Rickshaw* or *The City of Dreadful Night*—he will have something of value on his hands.

Where do we look for old books? You do not pick them up in Delhi or Bombay or Calcutta except at a very high price. There is more scope in the smaller towns, if you have the time and perseverance for a search. Many old club libraries have been broken up and dispersed. And in hill stations, old residents have gone away and sold their libraries for a song. Rummaging in the junk shops, I have found several interesting items on natural history for my personal library.

For the enthusiast willing to search in out-of-the-way places, there is still much to discover, provided the bookworms—a very real menace—have not got there first.

A bookworm (the real worm) has been defined as a 'maggot of sinister ancestry and predatory habits, particularly addicted to precious early books printed on good nourishing paper'. Bookworms are the life-long enemies of the collector, and there seems to be no way of getting rid of them.

in search of the perfect window

Those who advertise rooms or flats to let often describe them as 'room with bath' or 'room with tea and coffee-making facilities'. A more attractive proposition would be 'room with window,' for without a view a room is hardly a living place—merely a place of transit.

As an itinerant young writer, I lived in many single-room apartments, or 'bed-sitters' as they were called, and I have to admit that the quality of my life was certainly enhanced if any window looked out on something a little more inspiring than a factory wall or someone's backyard.

We cherish a romantic image of a starving young poet living in a garret and writing odes to skylarks, but, believe me, garrets don't help. For six months in London I lived in a small attic room that had no view at all, except for the roofs of other houses—an endless vista of gray tiles and blackened chimneys, without so much as a proverbial cat to relieve the monotony. I did not write a single ode, for no self-respecting nightingale or lark ever found its way up there.

My next room, somewhere near Clapham Junction, had a 'view of the railway,' but you couldn't actually see the railway lines because of the rows of washing that were hung out to dry behind the building.

It was a working-class area, and there were no laundries around the corner. But if you couldn't see the railway, you could certainly hear it. Every time a train thundered past, the building shuddered, and ornaments, crockery, and dishes rattled and rocked as though an earthquake were in progress. It was impossible to hang a picture on the wall; the nail (and with it the picture) fell out after a couple of days. But it reminded me a bit of my Uncle Fred's railway quarters just near Delhi's main railway station, and I managed to write a couple of train stories while living in this particular room.

Train windows, naturally, have no equal when it comes to views, especially in India, where there's an ever-changing panorama of mountain, forest, desert, village, town, and city—along with the colourful crowds at every railway station.

But good, personal windows—windows to live with—these were to prove elusive for several years. Even after returning to India, I had some difficulty finding the ideal window.

Moving briefly to a small town in northern India, I was directed to the Park View lodging house. There did happen to be a park in the vicinity, but no view of it could be had from my room or, indeed, from any room in the house. But I found, to my surprise, that the bathroom window actually looked out on the park. It provided a fine view! However, there is a limit to the length of time one can spend in the bath, gazing out at palm fronds waving in the distance. So I moved on again.

After a couple of claustrophobic years in New Delhi, I escaped to the hills, fully expecting that I would immediately find rooms or a cottage with windows facing the eternal snows. But it was not to be!

To see the snows I had to walk four miles from my lodgings to the highest point in the hill station. My window looked out on a high stone rampart, built to prevent the steep hillside from collapsing. True, a number of wild things grew in the wall—bunches of red sorrel, dandelions, tough weeds of various kinds, and, at the base, a large clump of nettles. Now I am sure there are people who can grow ecstatic over nettles, but I am not one of them. I find that nettles sting me at the first opportunity. So I gave my nettles a wide berth.

And then, at last, persistence was rewarded. I found my present abode, a windswept, rather shaky old house on the edge of a spur. My bedroom window opened on to blue skies, mountains striding away into the far distance, winding rivers in the valley below, and, just to bring me down to earth, the local television tower. Like the Red Shadow in 'The Desert Song,' I could stand at my window and sing 'Blue heaven, and you and I,' even if the only listener was a startled policeman.

The window was so positioned that I could lie on my bed and look at the sky, or sit at my desk and look at the hills, or stand at the window and look at the road below.

Which is the best of these views?

Some would say the hills, but the hills never change. Some would say the road, because the road is full of change and movement—tinkers, tailors, tourists, salesmen, cars, trucks and motorcycles, mules, ponies, and even, on one occasion, an elephant. The elephant had no business being up here, but I suppose if Hannibal could take them over the Alps, an attempt could also be made on the Himalayan passes. (It returned to the plains the next day.)

The road is never dull but, given a choice, I'd opt for the sky. The sky is *never* the same. Even when it's cloudless, the sky colours are different. The morning sky, the daytime sky, the evening sky, the moonlit sky, the starry sky, these are all different skies. And there are almost always birds in the sky—eagles flying high, mountain swifts doing acrobatics, cheeky myna birds meeting under the eaves of the roof, sparrows flitting in and out of the room at will. Sometimes a butterfuly floats in on the breeze. And on summer nights, great moths enter at the open window, dazzled by my reading light. I have to catch them and put them out again, lest they injure themselves.

When the monsoon rains arrive, the window has to be closed, otherwise cloud and mist fill the room, and that isn't good for my books. But the sky is even more fascinating at this time of the year.

From my desk I can, at this very moment, see the clouds advancing across the valley, rolling over the hills, ascending the next range. Raindrops patter against the window panes, closed until the rain stops.

And when the shower passes and the clouds open up, the heavens are a deeper, darker blue. Truly magic, casements these ... For every time I see the sky I am aware of belonging to the universe rather than to just one corner of the earth.

when the monsoon breaks

I was staying at a small hotel in Meerut, in north India. There had been no rain for a month, but the atmosphere was humid, and there were clouds overhead, dark clouds burgeoning with moisture. Thunder blossomed in the air.

The monsoon was going to break that day. I knew it; the birds knew it; the grass knew it. There was the smell of rain in the air. And the grass, the birds, and I responded to this odour with the same longing.

A large drop of water hit the windowsill, darkening the thick dust on the woodwork. A faint breeze had sprung up, and again I felt the moisture, closer and warmer.

Then the rain approached like a dark curtain. I could see it moving down the street, heavy and remorseless. It drummed on the corrugated tin roof and swept across the road and over the balcony of my room. I sat there without moving, letting the rain soak my sticky shirt and gritty hair.

Outside, the street rapidly emptied. The crowd disappeared. Then buses, cars, and bullock carts ploughed through the suddenly rushing water. A group of small boys, gloriously naked, came romping along a side street, which was like a river in spate. A garland of marigolds, swept off the steps of a temple, came floating down the middle of the road.

The rain stopped as suddenly as it had begun.

The day was dying, and the breeze remained cool and moist. In the brief twilight that followed, I was witness to the great yearly flight of insects into the cool, brief freedom of the night.

Termites and white ants, which had been sleeping through the hot season, emerged from their lairs. Out of every hole and crack, and from under the roots of trees, huge winged ants emerged, at first fluttering about heavily on this, the first and last flight of their lives. There was only one direction in which they could fly—toward the light—toward the street lights and the bright neon tube light above my balcony.

The light above my balcony attracted a massive, quivering swarm of clumsy termites, giving the impression of one thick, slowly revolving mass. A frog had found its way through the bathroom and came hopping across the balcony to pause beneath the light. All he had to do was gobble, as insects fell around him.

This was the hour of the geckos, the wall lizards. They had their reward for weeks of patient waiting. Plying their sticky pink tongues, they devoured insects as swiftly and methodically as children devour popcorn. For hours they crammed their stomachs, knowing that such a feast would not come their way again. Throughout the entire hot season the insect world had prepared for this flight out of darkness into light, and the phenomenon would not happen again for another year.

In hot up-country towns in India, it is good to have the first monsoon showers arrive at night, while you are sleeping on the veranda. You wake up to the scent of wet earth and fallen neem leaves, and find that a hot and stuffy bungalow has been converted into a cool, damp place.

The swish of the banana fronds and the drumming of the rain on broad-leaved sal trees will soothe any brow.

During the rains, the frogs have a perfect country-music festival. There are two sets of them, it seems and they sing antiphonal chants all evening, each group letting the other take its turn in the fairest manner. No one sees or hears them during the hot weather, but the moment the monsoon breaks, they swarm all over the place.

When night comes on, great moths fly past, and beetles of all shapes and sizes come whirring in at the open windows. The fireflies also light up their lamps, flashing messages to each other through the mango groves. Some nocturnal insects thrive mainly at the expense of humans, and sometimes one wakes up to find thirty or forty mosquitoes looking through the netting in a hungry manner. If you are sleeping out, you'll need that mosquito-netting.

The road outside is lined with fine babul trees, now covered with powdery little balls of yellow blossom, filling the air with a faint scent. After the first showers, there is a great deal of water about, and for many miles the trees are standing in it. The common sights along an up-country road are often picturesque—the wide plains, with great herds of smoke-coloured, delicate-limbed cattle being driven slowly home for the night, accompanied by troops of ungainly buffaloes, and flocks of goats and black long-tailed sheep. Then you come to a pond, where the buffaloes are indulging in a wallow, no part of them visible but the tips of their noses.

Within a few days of the first rain, the air is full of dragonflies, crossing and recrossing, poised motionless for a moment, then darting away with that mingled grace and power that is unmatched among insects. Dragonflies are the swallows of the insect world; their prey is the mosquitoes, the gnats, the midges, and the flies. These swarms, therefore, tell us that the moistened surface of the ground, with its mouldering leaves and sodden grass, has become one vast incubator teeming with every form of ephemeral life.

After the monotony of a fierce sun and dusty landscape quivering in the dim distance, one welcomes these days of mild, light, green earth, and purple hills coming near in the clear and transparent air.

And later on, when the monsoon begins to break up and the hills are dappled with light and shade, dark islands of clouds moving across the bright green sea, the effect on one's spirit is strangely exhilarating. For in India the true spring, the beginning of things, the birthday of nature, is not in March but in June.

in the darkness of the night

No night is so dark as it seems.

Here in Landour, on the first range of the Himalayas, I have grown accustomed to the night's brightness—moonlight, starlight, lamplight, firelight! Even fireflies and glow-worms light up the darkness.

Over the years, the night has become my friend. On the one hand, it gives me privacy; on the other, it provides me with limitless freedom.

Not many people relish the dark. There are some who will even sleep with their lights burning all night. They feel safer that way. Safer from the phantoms conjured up by their imaginations. A primeval instinct, perhaps, going back to the time when primitive man hunted by day and was in turn hunted by night.

And yet, I have always felt safer by night, provided I do not deliberately wander about on cliff tops or roads where danger is known to lurk. It's true that burglars and lawbreakers often work by night, their principal object being to get into other people's houses and make off with the silver or the family jewels. They are not into communing with the stars. Nor are late-night revellers, who are usually to be found in brightly lit places and are thus easily avoided. The odd drunk stumbling home is quite harmless and probably in need of guidance. I have often helped drunks find their way home, although I have yet to be thanked for it!

I feel safer by night, yes, but then I do have the advantage of living in the mountains, in a region where crime and random violence are comparatively rare. I know that if I were living in a big city in some other part of the world, I would think twice about walking home at midnight, no matter how pleasing the night sky.

Walking home at midnight in Landour can be quite eventful, but in a different sort of way. One is conscious all the time of the silent life in the surrounding trees and bushes. I have smelt a leopard without seeing it. I have seen jackals on the prowl. I have watched foxes dance in the moonlight. I have seen flying squirrels flit from one treetop to another. I have observed pine martens on their nocturnal journeys, and listened to the calls of nightjars and owls and other birds who live by night.

Not all on the same night, of course. That would be a case of too many riches all at once. Some night walks can be uneventful. But usually there is something to see or hear or sense. Like those foxes dancing in the moonlight. One night, when I got home, I sat down and wrote these lines:

As I walked home last night,
I saw a lone fox dancing
In the bright moonlight.
I stood and watched; then
Took the low road, knowing
The night was his by right.
Sometimes, when words ring true,
I'm like a lone fox dancing
In the morning dew.

Who else, apart from foxes, flying squirrels, and night-loving writers, are at home in the dark?

Well, there are the nightjars, not much to look at, although their large, lustrous eyes gleam uncannily in the light of a lamp. But their sounds are distinctive. The breeding call of the Indian nightjar resembles the sound of a stone skimming over the surface of a frozen pond; it can be heard for a considerable distance. Another species utters a loud grating call which, when close at hand, sounds exactly like a whiplash cutting the air. 'Horsfield's nightjar' (with which I am more familiar in Mussoorie) makes a noise similar to that made by striking a plank with a hammer.

During the day the bird spends long hours sitting motionless on the ground, where it is practically invisible, only springing into life when an intruder approaches. It is also called the 'Goatsucker' because of its huge mouth and the legend spread in many countries that it feeds from the udders of cows and goats. Because of this erroneous belief, it is considered a bird of ill omen. Night-flying insects, such as moths and beetles, are its preferred meals.

I must not forget the owls, those most celebrated of night birds, much maligned by those who fear the night.

Most owls have very pleasant calls. The little jungle owlet has a note which is both mellow and musical. One misguided writer has likened its call to a motorcycle starting up, but this is a libel. If only motorcycles sounded like the jungle owl, the world would be a more peaceful place to live and sleep in.

Then there is the little scops owl, who speaks only in monosyllables, occasionally saying 'Wow' softly but with great deliberation. He will continue to say 'Wow' at intervals of about a minute, for several hours throughout the night.

Probably the most familiar of Indian owls is the spotted owlet, a noisy bird who pours forth a volley of chuckles and squeaks in the early evening and at intervals all night. Towards sunset, I watch the owlets emerge from their holes one after another. Before coming out, each puts out a queer little round head with staring eyes. After they have emerged they usually sit very quietly for a time as though only half awake. Then, all of a sudden, they begin to chuckle, finally breaking out in a torrent of chattering. Having in this way 'psyched' themselves into the right frame of mind, they spread their short, rounded wings and sail off for the night's hunting.

I wind my way homewards. 'Night with her train of stars' is always enticing. The poet Henley found her so. But he also wrote of 'her great gift of sleep', and it is this gift that I am now about to accept with gratitude and humility. For it is also good to be up and dancing in the morning dew.

thoughts on reaching 75

The barbet calls from the top of the spruce tree.

Summer is here again.

The 75th summer of my life, although I have to admit that I don't remember the first five.

I remember an early summer in Jamnagar, paddling on the beach and staring out at a little steamer making its way across the Gulf of Kutch; an April morning in Dehradun, the air scented with mango blossom; a long hot summer in New Delhi, the bhisti splashing water on the khus-khus seed curtain (no air-conditioning then); a summer's day in Shimla, consuming ice-creams in the company of my father. All these summers before I was ten.

I was born early one morning in May, hence my prediliction for summer. There's nothing like the sun. In the plains it makes you more appreciative of the shade provided by leafy peepal and banyan trees. In the hills it brings you out of your chilly rooms to bask in its glory. Gardens need sunshine, and I need flowers, so we follow the sun together.

What have I learnt in these seventy-five years on planet earth? Quite frankly, very little. Don't believe the elders and philosophers. Wisdom does not come with age. It is born with you in the cradle. Either you have it or you don't. For the most part I have followed instinct rather than intelligence, and this has resulted in a modicum of happiness.

Happiness is as elusive as a butterfly, and you must never pursue it. If you stay very still, it might come and settle on your hand. But only briefly. Savour those precious moments, for they will not come your way very often.

Contentment is easier to attain. The best example is the small ginger cat who arrives on the balcony every afternoon, to curl up in the sun and slumber peacefully for a couple of hours. There's nothing like an afternoon siesta to help mind and body recuperate from the stress and toil of a busy morning. As Garfield would say: 'Some call it laziness. I call it deep thought.'

To have got to this point in life without the solace of religion says something for all the things that have brought me joy and a degree of contentment. Books, of course. I couldn't have survived without books. And living up here in the hills, where the air is sharp and clean, and you can look at your window and see the mountains marching away into the sunset or sunrise.

Dawn, daybreak, sunrise. They are all different. Twilight, dusk, nightfall. All quite different. We must be aware of these subtle differences in the light around us if we are to appreciate the life around us. There is no harm in sitting in an office and making money, but sometimes you must look out of the window. And look at the changing light. 'For the night has a thousand eyes and the day but one'. But the light of millions of lives is that fiery sun.

Happiness is also a matter of temperament, and temperament is something you are born with, acquired from near or distant ancestors. Unfortunately we cannot choose our ancestors, and often we are saddled with their worst traits—quarrelsome natures, unmanageable egos, envy, a tendency to grab what isn't ours ... 'The fault, dear Brutus, lies not in our stars but in ourselves that we are underlings ...' Shakespeare put his finger on it occasionally.

And luck, is there such a thing as luck? Some people seem to have all the luck. Or is that too a matter of temperament? A nature that doesn't sue for happiness often receives it in large measure. A nature that's placid, undemanding, does not suffer the same frustrations as do those who are impatient, ambitious, power-oriented.

Luck would seem to walk beside the healthy and those unencumbered by the daily struggle for survival. We try to summon up Lady Luck, but there are long periods when she stays away and we have to be patient and hope for her return. 'Luck, be my lady tonight!' sings the gambler in the Damon Runyon story, and once in a while she does smile upon us, albeit when least expected.

Luck and Chance are the same thing, I suppose. I have found that Chance gives, and takes away, and gives again. And so, when things are looking dark and gloomy, I know that daybreak is not far off.

I have been extremely fortunate or lucky or blessed by all the gods in that I have lived to this ripe age without too much disappointment or distress. I have made a fair living, doing the thing I enjoy most—putting words together and telling stories—and I have been able to find people to love and live for . . .

Was it all accidental, or was it ordained, or was it in my nature to arrive unharmed at this final stage of life's journey? I love this life passionately, and I wish it could go on and on. But all good things must come to an end, and when the time comes to make my exit, I hope I can do so with good grace and humour.